TWENTIETH-CENTURY PHILOSOPHY

TWENTIETH-CENTURY
PHILOSOPHY

BERNARD DELFGAAUW

Translated by
N. D. SMITH

MAGI BOOKS, INC.

33 Buckingham Drive   Albany, New York 12208

First published in English in 1969

Gill and Macmillan Ltd.
2 Belvedere Place
Dublin 1

Originally published as
De Wijsbegeerte van de 20e Eeuw
by Uitgeverij het Wereldvenster, Baarn, Holland

Library of Congress Catalogue Card No. 78-77165

SBN 87343-024-7

First published in the United States in 1969 by Magi Books, Inc.

Printed in the Republic of Ireland by Cahill and Company, Ltd. Dublin.

CONTENTS

PREFACE

This book begins with an outline of the backgrounds against which the problems of twentieth-century philosophy are set. This is followed by an account of the various answers that philosophers have given in this century to the questions put to them. Every philosopher, of course, gives his own answer and anyone who is involved with contemporary thought has to try to find the most important answers and to describe their essential features. I have therefore attempted to provide an insight into what twentieth-century philosophy is essentially concerned with. The reader who is interested in seeing how the philosophy of our own century is related to that of previous periods should consult the author's *Concise History of Philosophy*, Part 1 (Ancient and Medieval Philosophy) and Part 2 (Modern Philosophy).

Chapter 12 and half of Chapter 13 are based on the text which the author wrote for the fourth edition of Ferdinand Sassen's *Wijsbegeerte van onze tijd* (Antwerp and Amsterdam 1957), and this book is recommended to the reader who is anxious to obtain a more detailed treatment of the material and further biographical and bibliographical information.

HAARLEM, AUGUST 1957.

B. DELFGAAUW.

PREFACE TO THE SECOND EDITION

The text has been completely revised for this new edition. Rather more attention has been devoted to Dutch philosophy within the framework of the whole. Sassen's *Wijsgerig leven in Nederland in de 20e eeuw* (Amsterdam 1960) should be consulted for a more detailed treatment and for the philosophy of the idea of law in particular.

Various changes have also been made elsewhere in the book, especially in the chapter on Marxism. The title of Chapter 5, Part 3, has been altered. A brief review of the thought of Teilhard de Chardin has been added to the chapter on the philosophy of evolution. Finally, the index has been revised.

HAARLEM, AUGUST 1961.

B.D

PREFACE TO THE FOURTH EDITION

As in the third edition, no important changes have been made in this fourth edition. Only the dates have been revised.

HAARLEM, DECEMBER 1963.

B.D.

1 The Backgrounds

1. *The Historical Background*

There is continuity in thought. New thinking is new in that it is different from what has gone before and it is consequently linked with older thinking. Twentieth-century philosophy is a developing answer to the questions that mankind was asking itself at the end of the nineteenth century. Insofar as it is mankind that is involved here, the questions that are involved are, in a certain sense, questions that have been asked at all times. Insofar, however, as it is a historically situated mankind that is involved, what is involved is not mankind as such, but European man, and consequently a special way of questioning which is one possible way among others. We may be struck by the divergence of this questioning from that of the past, but we may also be struck by its convergence.

If we wish to understand the convergence, we must be alert to the mental sphere within which the philosophy has developed. It is the answer to a problem which is essentially metaphilosophical. This is because philosophy expresses a reality to which it is related, but with which it does not coincide. The point of departure for any understanding of the philosophical questioning of the twentieth century must be the situation itself, as it has presented itself to the thinkers who have given modern philosophy its form. This questioning has only to a very slight extent been determined by philosophy as developed during the second half of the nineteenth century. It has been dominated by realities that lie outside philosophy as such.

A very close relationship has existed between philosophy and positive science since the earliest beginnings of the history of European thought. The earliest Greek thought was both philosophical and scientific (natural science). A rapid development, however, soon led to a distinction being made between philosophy and special sciences such as mathematics, natural science and medicine. This *distinction* did not, however, lead to a *division* being made between philosophy and 'positive' science, and such distinction without division persisted until the Middle Ages. More important, though, than the relationship between philosophy and the special sciences at that time was the relationship between philosophy and Christian theology. Medieval thought was predominantly theological, although philosophy achieved more and more relative independence from theology within this theological framework of thought.

Towards the end of the Middle Ages, the positive sciences began to dissociate themselves from philosophy and philosophy in turn began to dissociate itself from theology. This twofold process of separation led to the emergence of a problem which even now still confronts European (and American) philosophy. Every form of contemporary philosophical thought provides either an implicit or an explicit answer to the question about its relationships with positive science on the one hand and theology on the other. What is more, theology and the positive sciences are also faced with the problem of their relationship with philosophy and with each other. In theology, these questions are asked quite explicitly, at least in the present century. In the positive sciences, they are for the most part only present implicitly, but it is becoming clear in the twentieth century that the leading exponents of the positive sciences are being forced to take up an explicit position. The problem is thus revealed in a very concrete form—is the physicist or the historian, who takes the 'philosophical' problem which he encounters into account, *still* a scientist or is he *already* a philosopher?

We are, of course, not at this stage concerned with how this problem arises in our own century, but with the background to the problem, that is, with how it presented itself in the second half of the nineteenth century. This can be indicated here only in broad outline and I shall therefore confine myself to the problem of those sciences which made the greatest contribution to the development of thought during that period, that is to say, the natural sciences (a term used to denote astronomy, physics and chemistry together), biology, psychology and the science of history.

We should also, by limiting ourselves in this way, be able to perceive the main features of the problem more easily. This limitation does not mean, of course, that such sciences as mathematics, economics and philology did not play an important part in this development. The part played by such sciences can, however, be indicated within the problem of those sciences mentioned in the preceding paragraph. Mathematics had an influence on the idea of being, for example, above all via the natural sciences. The discovery of non-Euclidic geometry certainly caused a great convulsion in the universal idea of being, but only once it had become 'concrete' in the natural sciences. Before this, non-Euclidic geometry seemed to most outsiders and perhaps even to many experts to be purely a game. It was not until the twentieth century that mathematics began to play an important part in other sciences such as biology, psychology and economics.

When Newton published his *Principia* in 1687, classical physics had already found its form. The process that led up to this has been described as the mechanization of man's image of the world. This process was, in principle, complete by 1687. This so-called mechanization began to be worked out, during the two centuries which followed, in the natural sciences and to have a continuous effect on the idea of being not only of those who practised these sciences, but also of those who did not take an active part in their development but lived in the sphere of thought within which they were developed. To a very great extent, it was this mechanization of man's view of the world that created the climate of thought which prevailed in the second half of the nineteenth century, a climate of thought which displayed certain features not foreseen or intended by Newton though they had nonetheless been partly determined by him.

The great success of classical physics caused an important change in man's attitude to the world. The world had always been ambiguous for him—sustaining and at the same time threatening and therefore incalculable. Now that the natural sciences and mathematics had found each other, however, nature had become in principle calculable and this new factor was furthermore strengthened by man's great progress in technical control of the world which the natural sciences made possible. Technology in the broadest sense of the word— including various trades, medicine and so on—was no longer simply the result of intuition, experience and chance, but was increasingly the product of a systematic knowledge of nature and, because it was systematic, this knowledge was also, in principle, capable of being developed more and more.

In this period, then, man became increasingly convinced that technology, in removing the threatening aspect from the world and enabling him to control his environment, would eventually transform his whole life. Even during the Enlightenment, but far more strongly in the nineteenth century, this conviction led to the idea of progress—that man was moving towards an era in comparison with which the whole of his previous history was insignificant. Scientific success was first and most clearly apparent in the spheres of physics and astronomy, and later in the field of chemistry. The mathematical method became more and more important and the belief that only mathematical science was genuine science rapidly gained ground. Authentic science was science in which the laws of 'dead' matter could be expressed in mathematical terms.

The great progress made in physics led to the conviction that the method used in physics was the only possible method. This in turn led to the belief that true science was practised only where this method prevailed and consequently that reality existed only where this science was able to develop. Thus materialism gained ground via a theoretical consideration and spread rapidly via man's existential experience. Technical progress disclosed a future in which all possible forms of human misery would eventually be removed and made men think that life in a world in which man had been freed from so much misery was the only one which they could expect. The 'other' world seemed to men of this period to be an imaginary one, a flight from reality. This flight from reality had been meaningful enough in the past, when life in this world had been unbearable, but it had clearly become an enemy of progress as soon as it had become apparent that human misery could, in principle, be entirely overcome.

The natural sciences were completely deterministic, maintaining an indissoluble causal connection between events, so that every later condition in nature could be calculated from the condition that preceded it. The conviction that this scientific method also applied to all reality resulted in the deterministic attitude being transferred from lifeless to living nature and then to man.

At this time, then, a resolute attempt was made to think of man as a determined being and of freedom as an illusion. This also resulted in the prevalence of materialism among scientists and philosophers and in the spread of materialism from these spheres to far wider circles in society. There was, however, continued active resistance to determinism and materialism, and in the second half of the nineteenth century especially thought was to a great extent conditioned by the antithesis between mind and matter, freedom and the absence of freedom.

This deterministic and materialistic attitude towards the world seemed to be confirmed by the developments that were taking place at this time in the field of biology. In 1859, Darwin's book, *On the Origin of Species,* gave, in a very striking way, great prominence to the idea of evolution which had already been expressed earlier. The natural sciences were shedding a great deal of light on lifeless nature, and at the same time the idea that different species of living beings had descended from others according to definite laws was strengthening man's understanding of the interconnections in all living nature. The idea of the 'struggle for life' also predominated in the work of many philosophers and was even incorporated in a special way into the classical economics of the period. It was a striking and attractive idea.

If there was unity in lifeless nature and unity in living nature, was there not a link between the two and, if so, where was it to be found? Did living nature not develop from lifeless nature and was it therefore, in principle and in essence, really distinct from lifeless nature? Such a theory gave new scope for materialism. Evolution also seemed to confirm the causal determinism of the whole of reality and to make the Cartesian idea of *bêtes-machines* more attractive. At the same time, it gave man a sense of solidarity with living nature which he felt impelled to elaborate further, in one way or another, in conceptual terms.

The same period also saw the emergence of experimental psychology as a distinct science, no longer directly associated with philosophy. Originally, of course, it was philosophers, like Wundt in Germany and Heymans in the Netherlands, who practised experimental psychology, but the psychologist who was no longer concerned with philosophy as such soon emerged as a special type. At this time too, a school of thought, usually designated by the term psychologism, achieved great prominence. The fundamental argument of psychologism was that the different aspects of human society, such as religion, philosophy and law, could all be traced back to psychology and completely understood in the light of psychology because they were simply and solely psychic structures. These thinkers directed their attention to the genesis of psychic phenomena, which they strove to understand within a natural connection of cause and effect.

The development of the science of history was also of fundamental importance. Like those of the natural sciences, the basic principles and the method of history as a modern science go back to the seventeenth century. By the nineteenth century, the science of history had achieved full maturity and was already exerting a deep influence on the thought of natural scientists and even on those who were not themselves engaged in the natural sciences, but in the study of literature and philology, in the social and juridical sciences and in philosophy and theology. Man came to regard the world as something that was constantly in motion and to be more interested in what was moving than in what was lasting and in the origin more than in the structure of reality.

The sciences of nature and of history were at one in their great respect for the *fact*. In both spheres, the fact was the only possible point of departure for a scientific description or argument. Despite Kant, the idea that a fact was only a fact within the framework of a definite theory, and therefore presupposed the activity of the human mind, was completely absent. On the basis of this assumption of the 'bare fact' and of this disregard for the activity of the human mind, the science of history could also be interpreted materialistically.

This historical awareness was reinforced by the rapidly

developing theory of evolution in biology, which was in turn only possible on the basis of the existence of such historical awareness. Biology was able to supply the link for an interpretation of history according to the pattern of the natural sciences. The historical event was, in other words, just as determined as the event in lifeless nature. This idea followed as a matter of course as soon as it was regarded as possible to view and understand man completely as a purely natural scientific phenomenon, since what applied to man as an individual was bound also to apply to the history of human society.

All the structures of human society were viewed historically and the historical explanation was regarded as the only possible explanation and at the same time as the only satisfactory one. Once the origin and development of a given structure—the language or the ethical consciousness of a certain group of people, for example—had been sufficiently demonstrated, there were no more questions to be asked. Once the way in which a structure had come about, its history, had been revealed, there was no need for further explanations. This led to a drawing back farther and farther from the horizon in order to find an ever more distant and favourable vantage-point from which to view the present structure or event. This historical awareness was of decisive importance to the development of many sciences, and of the history of religions, of philology and of palaeontology, because, even if it did not in fact create them, it certainly stimulated them to intense activity.

All this had a deep effect on European man's sense of being, making it increasingly relative. If every phenomenon had its history and if the earlier forms in which every structure appeared were different from those which appeared later, surely all these structures were relative? Was not man himself a relative being which arose at some point in the course of history, developed according to necessary laws, but which was essentially as unstable as any other phenomenon? The only stability which characterized man was that of matter, the pattern of which had already been revealed by the natural sciences. Everything that man displayed and everything that the human mind created was merely an attendant phenomenon of matter—a secretion of the brain, as the materialist philosophers of this period liked to call it.

Science is one of the most important realities in the light of which contemporary man's idea of being must be understood, but it is not the only theme that provides the backbround to this idea of being and to the philosophy arising from it. Other aspects of nineteenth-century thought form part of the background to the problem of contemporary philosophy. I have already mentioned the rapid advance of technology in connection with that of the natural sciences. This technological progress also had a far-reaching influence on the social situation, contributing largely to the emergence of the proletariat and consequently to the important social problem of the nineteenth century.

The thought of Karl Marx played an essential part in man's awareness of his social situation. Marx not only established convincingly that society was divided into classes, but also contributed to man's consciousness of this division by giving it great emphasis and presenting it as an extreme tension in society. The idea of progress was aroused by Marx's teaching in the minds of the workers, who were already beginning to feel that they were excluded from the world. Practical materialism, which, for the working class, was the result of its being excluded from everything to do with the mind and the spirit, was given a theoretical basis by Marx. According to his doctrine of historical materialism, the relationships of production were the motivating force in history—in other words, in human progress—and the result of this was that man's religious longing for individual and collective salvation was transformed in these relationships into an active desire for a salvation attainable in this world.

Marx thus posed the problem of a philosophy which aimed to change the world as against a philosophy which set out simply to consider the world. The predominant idea of the nineteenth century, however, continued to be that theory and practice should be kept distinct from each other. Man *understood* in philosophy and science, but he *acted* in the social and political forms which he gave to the world. The leading circles in Europe imposed their own forms on European society and went on to impose them on the whole of the world. Imperialism and colonialism did not look for any theoretical justification for their actions—although they tried sometimes to justify them afterwards in bad faith—and they were generally accepted as a matter of course simply because the superiority of Western man was taken for granted.

All this had grave repercussions on nineteenth-century religious thinking. The historical approach found its way into theology and religious thought and challenged the absolute claims of Christianity. The division of Christianity as a result of the Reformation had already exposed the Christian religion to the possibility of such a challenge. The historical study of comparative religion began in earnest and, to a very great extent, replaced theology. Even in the Enlightenment, the idea had been prevalent that everyone had to find God in his own way and that the different religions of the world were consequently all of equal value. Their differences were outward, historical differences. Essentially, they were one.

This recognition of the other religions of the world was apparently in conflict with Western man's feeling of superiority, but essentially this sense of superiority was based solely on his achievements in the positive sciences, in technology and in economics. The origin of these realities was never, in fact, subjected to critical and speculative review, with the result that the relationship between Western religiosity and Western science and technology never became apparent to nineteenth-century man. The prevalent materialism of the nineteenth century was also expressed in this, as it was in colonialism. Religion, separated from social and scientific life, became less and less meaningful in the life of the individual and of society as a whole; it gave no guidance either to the worker or to the scientist, both of whom were looking for a new world.

Philosophy's contribution to the idea of being at this time was very slight. Of the three great figures in the field of philosophy, Kierkegaard and Nietzsche had, as yet, no influence. Marx rapidly began to exert a wide influence, but this was, for the time being, principally confined to the political sphere. The leading circles of this period felt little or no need for deeper philosophical speculation. Consciously or unconsciously, their thinking was determined mainly by Comte's positivism, which—although it was not in any sense intended as materialism—seemed to lend itself most easily to the materialistic and historical aspirations of the period.

It would, however, be wrong to take only the continued effect and elaboration of positivism into account in the philsophy of the second half of the nineteenth century. There were other tendencies at work, although these had little influence outside their own limited circles because their significance was not apparent to the prevalent thought of the time. The spiritualism of Maine de Biran continued to be felt in France and was effective in various directions (Lequier, Lagneau, Ravaisson and Lachelier). Newman was active in England and, in Germany, the first foundations were being laid for a philosophy of values (Lotze) and for phenomenology (Bolzano and Brentano). For the time being, however, little attention was given to these philosophical tendencies, just as Marx, Kierkegaard and Nietzsche were temporarily relegated to the fringe of philosophy and regarded as interesting only within the spheres of politics, economics and literature.

It was, above all, this general flatness which made some people realize that it was necessary to return to the great philosophers of the past. Men who were principally concerned with a philological study of the Greek philosophers became at the same time interested in their greatness as thinkers—for example, Jowett in his study of Plato and Trendelenburg in his examination of Aristotle. Others thought that there was a possibility of deepening contemporary philosophy by returning to Thomas Aquinas, Kant or Hegel. Kant was rediscovered in Germany and Hegel in England, Italy and the Netherlands. This prepared the way for what was radically to determine the thinking of the first quarter of the twentieth century and was to continue to be of fundamental importance in the whole of contemporary thought.

2. The Present Background

There is a dividing line somewhere between the thought of the nineteenth century and that of the twentieth. This division does not, of course, coincide exactly with the year 1900, but it is generally agreed that the spirit of thought in the twentieth century is different from that in the nineteenth century. There is disagreement only about the time that this change took place. Many of those who have considered this phenomenon are inclined to think that the dividing line should be placed at the outbreak of the First World War in 1914. Others put it before or after this date. It is perhaps better not to look too closely for a dividing line at all, but simply to be alert to the fact that thought did take a different direction and that the first indications of this new direction were already apparent before the end of the nineteenth century.

The change took place in all spheres of society—in science,

philosophy and theology, in art and technology, in social relationships, politics and religion. In order to throw light on this change of direction, I shall once again take some of the most important aspects of science as my starting-point. The most fundamental point to notice here is not the development within each separate science, but the convergence of the various sciences despite increasing specialization. To put it briefly, the nineteenth-century dream of one united science in accordance with the natural scientific method was not realized, but its failure opened the way for a comprehensive view of the world. Natural science was no longer opposed to history as the last territory that it had to try to conquer. In a certain sense, it became history, just as history also in a certain sense became natural science. In this process, biology began to play an extremely important part.

Modern man's idea of being is to a very great extent determined by natural science and history. In both of these sciences, the change of direction to which I have referred took place round about the turn of the century or at least began to show itself for the first time at this period. As far as the natural sciences are concerned, we can even give a date—that of the turn of the century itself. It was in 1900 that Max Planck proposed the quantum theory in physics, which set afoot the new trend of scientific thought which was to lead from the classical idea to the modern idea of natural science. Traditional natural science was not ended by this new tendency, but included in a broader perspective in which it remained valid with regard to the reality that it had in the past successfully investigated, but was regarded as invalid with regard to the 'deeper and further levels' of the reality to which natural science was beginning to turn its attention.

The classical physical concepts of causality and determination lost their unlimited validity. These concepts seemed to operate only within a definite sphere and even then their theoretical basis raised problems in connection with which a philosophical aspect presented itself as well as a natural scientific aspect. This caused the disappearance of the suggestion that natural science necessarily implied a denial of human freedom. If determinism was not valid in the case of lifeless nature, or at least if it was not demonstrable in certain situations, how, then, could it be affirmed *a priori* that it was valid in the case of living nature and man? However different the indeterminacy of certain physical processes and that of freedom might be, the discovery of the first provided space and latitude for the second.

Classical natural science had been guided by a definite idea of what understanding was. Something that could be understood was something that was conceivable. Determinism was, in one way or another, conceivable. If determinism could no longer be defined, then conceivability and thus the current mode of understanding were lost. In astronomy, conceivability was lost because it was necessary to appeal to non-Euclidic geometry. This gave great prominence to the questions that were evoked in a particularly urgent manner by Einstein's theory of relativity. What were time, space and movement? A new mode of understanding became necessary.

Natural scientists were consequently faced with a number of questions which were, by tradition, philosophical. This gave philosophy a new, topical importance—it became more than purely superfluous speculation, as it had been regarded in the immediate past. The physicist began to wonder not only what understanding was, but also whether he really understood at all. Was his scientific work not really a working with nature rather than an understanding of nature? If the macro-processes took place according to recognizable laws, while the micro-processes seemed to be exempt from those laws, did he really understand or was he simply predicting on the basis of statistical laws? The probability of prediction seemed to be replacing the certainty of understanding.

There was, however, another factor which played a part in this. Classical natural science developed the image of a universe that was necessary as it was. The point of departure for this view was the cosmos as inhabited and known by us. This point of departure was in itself intelligible. If another cosmos existed, it would have to have the same basic structure. This meant that the structure of this cosmos was more important than its history. Modern natural scientists were, however, struck by this history, which was a factual history, and not preoccupied with intelligibility, because even the structure departed from the classical mode of understanding. The cosmos was no longer a cosmos, a reality that happened to exist alongside other identical possibilities. The cosmos was *this* cosmos, which had its own unique character on the basis of its own history and structure.

This, in principle, bridged the gap between science and history. Biology, which had, in the preceding period, seemed to form the link by means of which all historical sciences could be reduced to natural sciences, now showed itself to be the link again, but in a different manner. Both the natural scientific aspect and the historical aspect were revealed in biology, so that this science was admirably suited to the task of illuminating both the historical aspects of nature and the natural scientific aspects of history. Biology had to accomplish this in fact by developing further the idea of evolution. A purely deterministic explanation of evolution came up against many difficulties. There seemed to be something like an internal finality of life, a distinctive structure of the living being. An explanation along the lines of current natural scientific thought could be provided for this as far as the individual parts of the living being were concerned, but not as far as life as a whole was concerned. As the research conducted by Driesch and others had shown, life displayed itself as a structure that was more than the sum of its parts.

Biologists had to try to understand this situation in the appropriate manner, with the result that the question as to what understanding really was also occurred to them. Just as sociology had proved to be necessary to the study of man's history, so too did sociological and historical problems present themselves to biologists. Lamarck and Darwin had already encountered these problems. Now, however, they arose in an increasingly complicated form. This was because evolutionists were no longer simply required to define the place of the animal and the various species of animal life in the history of living beings. They were also faced with the need to define, in a structural manner, the present place of a given species of animal with regard to other species in the animal kingdom, the vegetable world, climate, soil and man. Von Uexküll's concept of the *Umwelt*, the surrounding world or environment, was the structural counterpart of the concept of evolution.

This brings us to an essential aspect of the development of very different sciences in connection with the change of direction that took place round about the turn of the century. Classical natural science had always been concerned with the quest for causal connections. This quest was now taken over by entirely different branches of science, including history. The search has not been abandoned in this century, despite all the changes that have taken place in modern man's ideas of causality and determinism. Man's interest in the genesis of phenomena has, however, found a counterpart in his interest in their structure. On the one hand, we are aware not only that the historical origin and development of phenomena are of fundamental importance to our understanding and 'manipulation' of reality, but also that their present structure is equally important. On the other hand, we also realize that the present structure of phenomena, either in the present or in the past, has a logical precedence, since we have to know *what* we are investigating before we can trace its genesis.

Philology provides a striking example of this development. The historical and comparative study of languages originated in the nineteenth century, when even comparative philology had a historical orientation and was concerned with the problems of tracing various languages back to one single origin. Linguistic laws were defined according to the pattern of natural laws—the discovery of various phenomena in the field of phonetics in particular seemed to be admirably suited to this purpose. The merits of this historically orientated philology were very great and the results of research carried out in the nineteenth century in this field are, in many respects, of lasting importance. But twentieth-century philologists have also been interested in that aspect of the development of languages which cannot be understood as determined—they tend to see language as an aspect of man's being, and claim that the whole structure of this being can be discovered in language. Structural philology was developed at the very beginning of this century by de Saussure, who put forward the synchronic as against the diachronic theory of language. The first takes precedence over the second, since the present structure of a language has to be understood before its genesis can be investigated as a real linguistic genesis.

A similar development is also apparent in psychology. The theories of depth psychology, as first projected by Freud and later developed by, among others, Jung and Adler, are still, it is true, based entirely on the initial assumption of the validity of causality and determinism, but, in its essence, the study of depth psychology is entirely directed towards the structure of the human psyche. There is consequently a remarkable discrepancy between the insights of depth psychology, its practice and its theoretical justification. Whereas it is, in its theory, still deeply indebted to the nineteenth century, it has, as far as its essential inspiration is concerned, prepared the way for the development of a type of twentieth-century psychology that has an entirely different orientation. This new psychology does not neglect the genesis of the human psyche, but it places the emphasis on the present structure of the psyche. Although its point of departure is deterministic, it will have to make an increasingly serious appeal to human freedom.

Phenomenological psychology, which was developed later under the inspiration of Husserl, is a structural psychology which stresses man's unity and his solidarity with the world, as against the tendency in nineteenth-century psychology to regard man as a collection of separate faculties. This latter psychological view of man had already been overcome earlier in the twentieth century by the *Gestalt* psychologists, who prepared the way for an understanding of the unity of man and animal. The developments in *Gestalt* and phenomenological psychology are analogous to what has taken place in the field of biology during this century. Dilthey's theory of understanding has been of essential importance in the case of twentieth-century psychology and Driesch's view of the irreducibility of the living being has been fundamental in the case of biology.

Like the modern natural scientists, historians have also come to realize that the practice of science is not simply the registration of facts and their embodiment in laws. Something real is not a fact until it acquires significance for a certain theory, either because it confirms this theory or because it undermines it. Historians are now aware that not everything is of equal importance to history—that history is selective. This has made them wonder whether it is really so purely descriptive as it was believed to be in the nineteenth century. Precisely because of its selectivity, does it not determine the future as much as it describes the past? History cannot be separated from the person of the historiographer—its 'objectivity' is tied to its writer's being and is consequently, in a certain sense, 'subjective'. But the concepts of objectivity and subjectivity need to be more deeply thought out, because the traditional antithesis between object and subject applies as little to the science of history as it does to the modern natural sciences, in which the phenomenon of the influence of the perceiver on what is perceived has been clearly revealed.

This phenomenon is apparent in various ways in the different sciences. It is extremely evident in sociology and psychology, but it is equally valid in the field of medical science and practice. It is one of the aspects of psychosomatic medicine, a science which emerged late in the twentieth century, but only after a very long period of preparation. It is a science not only concerned with the interaction between the perceiver and what is perceived and with the establishment of a deeper and more fundamental relationship between the doctor and the patient, in which the whole of man's attitude towards the world is at issue. It is also concerned with the relationship between body and psyche. Medicine has become conscious of the same problem as psychology—man as a totality. This means that it has become necessary to re-examine the concepts of spirit, soul, mind, consciousness and body.

These new insights to which medical science has come are therefore similar to those of modern history. In both sciences, the relationship between the perceiver and what is perceived is being developed. In this process, history has been confronted by another science which originated in the nineteenth century, but which did not reach full maturity until the present century —sociology. We have become aware of the fact that a historical description of any form of genesis has to be preceded by an analysis of the structure of the phenomenon concerned. We want to know, if the growth of a certain human community or civilization is described by history, what a community or a civilization really is. Sociologists attempt to throw light on these structures and they have in fact made it clear that different forms of community and civilization are possible. They have also shown that the development of every form of science and indeed the growth of every human phenomenon presuppose a definite structure of society.

If all these tendencies in twentieth-century science are considered as a whole, it is quite obvious that the attitude of modern scientists towards nineteenth-century scientific thought cannot be regarded as uniform. The new scientific way of thinking is not simply opposed to that of the preceding period. The pattern of thesis and antithesis cannot be applied mechanically in this case and any attempt to regard contemporary science as a synthesis of the scientific thought of the nineteenth century and of an even earlier period would not be taking all the phenomena fully into account. In certain decisive cases, twentieth-century science merely continues in the direction taken by the nineteenth century. In others, however, it takes an entirely new direction.

Perhaps the most important way in which modern thought manifests continuity with the past is to be seen in its maintenance of the tendency to look at phenomena from the historical point of view. Twentieth-century man is no less historical in his thinking than nineteenth-century man, but his historical thinking has undoubtedly undergone a change. In the first place, he has learnt to appreciate that every attempt to throw light on a genesis must be preceded by a clarification of a structure. In the second place, he now realizes that history is not determined—it is human development, in which the two aspects of determinism and freedom are both present. There is a definite direction in human history from which no one can depart, but the form given to this direction and the position taken up with regard to it are matters of human freedom.

The relativization resulting from this historical tendency also plays a part in twentieth-century thought. The question as to whether relativity presupposes some form of absoluteness is, however, posed more sharply in the twentieth century than in the past. Einstein did not in any sense affirm, in his theory of relativity, that everything was relative—the theory was rather an attempt to find an absolute. Even a theory which maintains that everything is relative betrays a tendency towards absoluteness, so that the absolute seems to be inescapable. The question which arises in every sphere of thought today, including theology, is, what is the relationship between the absolute and the relative.

Compared with the thinking of the previous period, our thinking is new in its attempts to find unity. Nineteenth-century thinkers emphasized analysis and were inclined to regard what was analysed—the molecule, the living being, man or the community—as the sum of its parts. We, on the other hand, stress the unity of what is analysed, which cannot be understood as a sum of its parts, but as something that has its own structure. We tend to regard man, for example, as more than a collection of passions and faculties. The problem of freedom has thus arisen again in an acute form and material-ism has come to be regarded as insufficient. Man's unity and freedom have become central problems of the twentieth century, not only in philosophy, but also in theology, sociology, psychology, medical science and biology and even in physics.

The search for the genesis of phenomena has not been abandoned, but is now conducted at a different level. Twentieth-century man seeks the genesis of total structures and does not attempt to describe these structures historically as in the past. There is a renewed quest for the 'essential'. This has led to a crisis and a reorientation in the sciences. Each individual science is looking for its foundations which are, on the one hand, determined by the reality towards which it is directed and, on the other hand, conditioned by the specific manner in which it approaches its own sphere of activity. This search for foundations has brought the various sciences into contact with each other and with philosophy. The unity of all thought has thus become a question of central importance.

The background to philosophical thought is, however, no more dominated exclusively by science in our own time than it was in the nineteenth century. Religion, social relationships, politics and technology play just as important a part. This emerges with particular clarity in twentieth-century thinking about human progress. Twentieth-century man does not share the optimism of nineteenth-century man with regard to progress. His attitude towards progress has far more light and shadow. Many scientists, philosophers, theologians and artists have completely rejected the idea of progress and either regard the downfall of mankind as imminent or are convinced that all things, in their nature, remain unchanged. A second large group regards all thought about progress or retrogression as useless speculation and a third group is concerned with the conditions under which progress can in fact be discussed.

The reasons for this change in attitude are not in the first place to be found in the crisis through which the sciences have been passing, a crisis which may very well be regarded as progress, although it has in fact frequently been interpreted, but not by science as such, as a symptom of decline. The reasons must rather be sought in the ambivalent character of technology, in political development, in the economic crisis and in religious thought.

Science and technology were the glory of man in the period before the twentieth century, but the ambiguity of technology has become more and more clearly visible in our own times and this ambiguity is also, in a certain sense, apparent in science. This ambiguous element in technology was certainly revealed even in the nineteenth century, but it was either not seen or else explained away. At that time, it was revealed in the creation of the proletariat, but the prevalent attitude among the leading circles in nineteenth-century society was that this proletariat was not a threat to mankind, but a necessary secondary phenomenon of man's development. It might be an enduring phenomenon or it might be purely transient, but in any case it was not a possible disaster and, in the last resort, it did not essentially affect man's progress. The twentieth-century idea of progress is, however, quite different from that of the nineteenth century, when progress was experienced as that of one class in one part of the world. We now look upon progress only as that of the whole of mankind.

Although social relationships have certainly improved a great deal in the twentieth century, the economic crisis of the nineteen-thirties shattered man's confidence in progress. To this can be added the subsequent increasing realization that prosperity is a real concept only for a very small part of the world. The emergence of this realization has been a convincing proof to others that there is real progress, but that progress has to be interpreted differently from in the past.

There is also a very close link between the socio-economic sphere and that of politics. Nineteenth-century man dreamed of lasting world peace under the supreme mastery of Europe. The twentieth century has witnessed the destruction of this dream. There has been no real peace since the outbreak of the First World War. Europe's supremacy has been undermined as a result of two world wars and a very unstable balance has been established between two great powers which are quite differently orientated in their socio-economic, political and religious attitudes. Situated between these two powers, Europe has lost its dominant political and economic importance and nineteenth-century imperialism and colonialism have collapsed in a very short space of time.

The idea of decline in Europe is so widespread in the twentieth century that it is worth mentioning that Greek

c

thought first began to exert a deep influence on the known world when Greece herself had ceased to be a political power. Many thinkers today, however, are convinced not simply of the decline of Europe, but of the approaching downfall of mankind as a whole, and regard the two world wars as the preparation for this downfall and the present tension between East and West as its beginning. Others believe that this world-wide tension is the first indication of a unity of mankind that is so real that not only all forms of colonialism, but also all war will be impossible within it.

This conviction has not arisen from any belief that man has become more moral. It is based on the idea that, because war has become more and more a question of total mutual destruction, peace has thus become a simple question of self-preservation. This peace, however, only seems to be possible on the basis of a certain unity of thinking, which is not yet even distantly visible. This in turn leads to two possible points of view—on the one hand, that this unity of thinking and consequently peace are unattainable and, on the other, that it is in principle possible, despite all the tensions that exist in the world today, to achieve a certain unity. The ultimate conclusion of the first point of view is that mankind and the world are approaching downfall: that of the second is that self-preservation is forcing men towards *rapprochement*.

This explains modern man's sense of the ambivalence of technical progress. He can no longer accept technical progress viewed in isolation as human progress because he is sharply aware of both the constructive and the destructive aspects of technology. He freely admits that, in its constructive aspect, technology is able to promote human progress and indeed that it is absolutely indispensable to mankind and provides the only means of raising the level of prosperity among the under-developed nations. But this constructive aspect of technology often lags behind the advances made by technology as a destructive power, which can retard human progress and even destroy mankind.

The problem of technology therefore raises the whole question of human freedom. Technology itself does not act—it is man who acts in his utilization of technology. Technology confronts man with his responsibility as a human being. Especially since the end of the Second World War, an aspect of technology of which nineteenth-century man was hardly aware has thus been brought sharply to the fore—the technologist is not simply and solely a technologist, he is a man, and, as a man, he is responsible for what technology 'does'. What is more, since modern technology has become almost exclusively scientific technology, this responsibility falls above all on the shoulders of those who practise the natural sciences. Twentieth-century physicists and other natural scientists do not try to avoid this responsibility and again and again they appeal to the conscience of the world—something that would have been unthinkable in the nineteenth century.

This throws light from a new direction on the problem to which I have already alluded, that of the unity of reality. The natural sciences, freedom, and ethics are not isolated from each other and even biology and medicine are involved in the dialogue, which also has its scientific, humane and political aspects. Furthermore, a certain development has also reached its fulfilment in this century—the scholar has become the one who conducts war. But the scholar's conscience is not compliant here and does not allow him to accept this role easily, now that he has come to realize that his positive attitude to scientific progress is being changed into a negative attitude, directed towards wilful destruction.

Generally speaking, creative artists became aware of this development before philosophers. The essence of the problem can be found even in the work of Dostoyevski, and the belief that modern politics threaten to lead to the total mechanization of man emerged later in the novels of Kafka. As long ago as this, then, the whole problem of order in a planned society was revealed. In our own time, there is an almost universal acceptance of the idea that order does not come about automatically, as nineteenth-century man was inclined to believe, but that it must be created in planning. Planning is necessary, but it is also dangerous, because it contains a threat to what twentieth-century man has come to regard as the essence of his being—freedom. This has resulted in the emergence, during the course of this century, of the urgent question of the necessary relationship between planned order and human freedom. This problem is acute not only in the socio-economic and political spheres, but also in morals and religion, in the philosophical and theological spheres.

The development of religion has been quite different from what would have been regarded as possible in the nineteenth century. There has been, of course, an enormous decline among the mass of the people, but the problem of religion has again become vital in the leading circles of society. The change from orthodoxy to liberal thought in religion has not continued. On the contrary, religious thinkers are now convinced that it is necessary to go back to the early sources of religious inspiration. Not only dialogue between the different Christian confessions, but also dialogue between Christianity and the other world religions has led to a deeper understanding and thus to greater originality. All this has also resulted in a revival of Christian theology in the twentieth century. Theologians are no longer preoccupied, as they were in the nineteenth century, with the 'history of dogma', but have come to see their task as a speculation about the faith of Christians today and its connection, via tradition, with the faith of the first Christians. In the field of theology, then, there is also unity of structure and genesis. This revival was first experienced in the Protestant world, with the dialectical theology of Karl

Barth, Emil Brunner and others. In was followed by a similar revival in Catholic thinking. The so-called 'new theology' is one of the forms taken by this twentieth-century renewal in Catholic theology.

The echo of all this can be heard in philosophy. Twentieth-century philosophers have rediscovered the importance of the great and neglected thinkers of the nineteenth century, especially Kierkegaard and Nietzsche, and have given philosophy a deeper meaning by re-examining the work of the leading philosophers of all periods—Plato, Aristotle, Plotinus, Augustine, Thomas Aquinas, Descartes, Pascal, Kant and Hegel. After the stagnation of philosophical thought during the second half of the nineteenth century, our own century provides a pattern of philosophical speculation that is both richly varied and at the same time very profound. Philosophy has made a fresh encounter with religious thinking and theology. It is engaged in dialogue with science, but is no longer dependent on science, as it was in the nineteenth century. It is conscious of its responsibility towards the world and listens attentively to what creative art and literature have to say to it. It is no longer a philosophy that believes that it can understand everything, but a speculation that attempts to penetrate as deeply as possible into a reality which, in the last resort, it is incapable of grasping.

In the remaining chapters of this book, I shall try to provide an outline of the answers which twentieth-century philosophy has endeavoured to give to the problems with which it is confronted. Modern philosophy has a great diversity, and therefore a richness, but it also has a unity in its orientation, and therefore a depth. Some of the answers supplied by contemporary philosophy have been quite emphatically inspired by one or other philosopher of the past. Others owe less to earlier thinkers. Because of this, I have made a distinction between the philosophical tendencies which are to a great extent based on the thought of a particular philosopher of the past and those which are not. It is, of course, impossible to make a complete distinction of this kind because all the modern philosophical tendencies aim to provide an answer to the problems of our own age and all are at the same time in one way or another indebted to the past. The titles of Part 2 (Answers from Tradition) and Part 3 (Answers from the Change of Direction) should therefore be understood with this reservation in mind.

A more analytical treatment of the material dealt with in the following chapters and biographical and bibliographical data will be found in F. Sassen's *Wijsbegeerte van onze tijd*, Antwerp 1957.

A review of the themes in modern philosophy will be found in the symposium edited by F. Heinemann, *Die Philosophie im 20. Jahrhundert*, Stuttgart 1959.

The contrasts in contemporary philosophy are underlined by J. Ferrater-Mora in *Philosophy Today, Conflicting Tendencies in Contemporary Thought*, New York 1960.

The different movements in twentieth-century philosophy are reviewed by A. Weber and D. Huisman in *Tableaci de la philosophie contemporaire*, Paris 1957, and this book is particularly good in its discussion of French thought. In general, however, its treatment of philosophy outside France is quite insufficient, although there are chapters on English idealism, Husserl and German existentialism.

For the first part of the twentieth century a very illuminating book is H. de Vleeschauer's *Stroomingen in de hedendaagsche wijsbegeerte*, Antwerp 1932.

2 Answers from Tradition

When it became apparent, towards the end of the nineteenth century, that problems with which the philosophy of that time was not capable of dealing were arising in the world and in science, there was a revival in philosophy. This revival came from two different directions—there were those who looked for an entirely new thinking and those who sought to renew past thinking, looking quite emphatically for support from the past to provide an answer to the questions posed by the present. By studying and applying the philosophical principles of one of the great thinkers of the past, they attempted to find a solution for the new problems of the present. The most important thinkers whose writings were studied at this time were Thomas Aquinas, Kant, Hegel and Marx. This does not mean to say that other great figures in the history of philosophy were neglected. Interest in their work did not, however, lead to the formation of an important and influential school of thought—this only happened in the case of the four philosophers mentioned above. Wherever a school that was based on the thought of other philosophers was formed, it did not exert very much influence on the development of philosophy in the twentieth century. There is consequently no need to devote much space to such schools. Something that must, however, be mentioned explicitly is that some philosophers of the past—notably Plato, Aristotle, Plotinus, Augustine, Descartes, Pascal, Kierkegaard and Nietzsche—have had a very profound influence on twentieth-century thinking, without actually leading to the development of a specific movement in philosophy.

Wherever schools of thought did come about, however, there was no question of a flight from the problems of the contemporary world. On the contrary, every attempt was made to lead thought, by a process of education, into direct confrontation with these problems. The old saying, *Amicus Plato, sed magis amica Veritas,* was sometimes forgotten, but at least this forgetfulness was not stated as a principle. The aim was to obtain, via the thought of the philosopher chosen, a deeper and wider insight into truth and reality. The educative character of this return to the past is revealed quite clearly by the development of the different schools that were formed. Once the aim of bringing about a philosophical confrontation with the problems of the present had been achieved, the school lost its scholastic character and disappeared or else retained its unity simply because of its shared basic inspiration. The neo-Hegelian school disappeared in the first quarter of the twentieth century and the neo-Kantian school disappeared in the second quarter of the century. At the same period, neo-Thomism, which had initially been very closed, became extremely open. Marxism too showed signs of losing its closed attitude and, although it has produced very few creative figures, it has had a considerable influence on contemporary philosophy by keeping philosophical interest in the ideas of Marx alive.

1. *Neo-Thomism*

The term neo-Thomism is used in different senses and is indeed often rejected altogether. In the movement which began in the nineteenth century as a return to Thomas Aquinas, a distinction is frequently made between Thomism and neo-

Thomism. Here, however, the whole of this movement is referred to as neo-Thomism and the term Thomism is reserved for the original movement—the scholasticism of the High and Later Middle Ages. It is also a matter of less importance that neo-Thomism forms part of a much wider movement, neo-scholasticism, which contains not only a Thomist tendency, but also a Scotist and a Suarezian tendency. Within the whole movement, thought is principally concentrated in neo-Thomism, so that a description of the neo-Thomist position will indicate with sufficient clarity the place of neo-scholasticism.

Those who adhere to neo-Thomism as a philosophical movement are almost without exception Catholic thinkers, though even among them neo-Thomism is not universally accepted. The first attempts to renew Thomism were made by Italian philosophers early in the nineteenth century. Similar attempts were made later in Germany. But the movement was given its first real impetus by Pope Leo XIII, who, in his encyclical *Aeterni Patris* of 1879, warmly recommended the philosophy and theology of Thomas Aquinas to Catholic philosophers and theologians. Further steps gave additional stimulus to the neo-Thomist movement. The most important of these were the foundation of the San Tommaso Academy, Leonina's critical edition of the works of St Thomas and the establishment of a chair at Louvain for Thomist studies, to which DÉSIRÉ MERCIER (1851–1926) was appointed. The popes who succeeded Leo XIII continued to recommend Thomism in later documents.

It is necessary to go a little more deeply into the background in the Church and into Leo XIII's attitude. Leo was very familiar with the thought of his own time and clearly understood its significance. In Church circles generally, there was a pronounced tendency to reject science or at least a general attitude of anxiety with regard to it. Leo, on the other hand, was fully aware of its far-reaching implications, of the extent to which the character of the modern world was determined by it and of its importance to modern man as an orientation towards truth. He had consequently always encouraged the practice of science.

Unlike most of his contemporaries in the Church, Leo also appreciated that there was somewhere an intrinsic link between science and philosophy on the one hand and between philosophy and theology on the other. But in all three spheres, the part played by Catholics was very small—they were not making a very large contribution to the positive sciences, their share in philosophy was negligible and, in theology, they had more or less come to a dead end. In this critical situation, Leo looked for a point of contact in the past, a point at which Catholic thinkers had defined the development of philosophy and theology. He found this in the thought of Thomas Aquinas, which had already been given considerable prominence for some time by the Italian and German neo-Thomists.

Leo certainly had no intention of making Aquinas the foundation for the practice of philosophy and theology within Catholic circles and even less intention of tying the Catholic practice of science to Thomist thought. He simply wished to find a way of thinking which was broad and deep enough to give a new impetus to the stagnating Catholic thought of his own time and what he had in mind was, in the first place, the training of priests and, in the second place, a revival of philosophy and theology as such within the Church. This twofold aim is clearly expressed in the papal documents. Thomism—or at least scholasticism—was prescribed for the seminaries in which future priests were trained. Outside the seminaries, it was strongly recommended, but not made obligatory. This distinction has, since then, always been preserved.

It is quite understandable that the Pope's first concern should have been for the training of priests. It was becoming more and more obvious that a good philosophical and theological education was indispensable to the modern priest. It was also clear that the seminaries seldom satisfied this requirement. Seminary teachers were unable to find their way in the problems of the modern age and for the most part what they taught was an eclectic philosophy and theology containing scholastic, Cartesian and idealistic elements. It was becoming more and more apparent that this eclecticism was completely inadequate and that seminary instruction needed above all to be inspired by a thinker who was able to give both philosophy and theology its own distinctive character.

Naturally enough, the Church could hardly look for this inspiration anywhere else but within her own tradition. Leo XIII consequently went back to Thomas, with whose work he had already become acquainted as a student. His aim was to train future priests in a spirit that was both thoroughly philosophical and theological and at the same time deeply Catholic. Clearly, it was impossible to find a post-medieval thinker who satisfied these demands. Thomas, whose thought combined philosophy and theology in a unity that preserved their separate identities, was obviously a better choice than any other traditional Christian thinker. Augustine was no less profound in his thinking than Thomas, but he lacked the synthetic grasp which characterized Thomas's thought and which was so important in any introductory instruction in philosophy and theology.

Neo-Thomism could not, however, simply be a repetition, without any problems, of Thomism. On the one hand, classical Thomism had never become, either in the case of Thomas himself or in the case of those who followed Thomas, a finished system. On the other hand, neo-Thomism was required to review an entirely new situation, within which questions were raised which were quite different from those presented by the situation within which Thomas himself had provided his answers. First and foremost, there was the problem of the relationship between philosophy and theology. Leo XIII asked for a Thomist philosophy to be practised. But did such a philosophy really exist? Thomas had certainly formulated the principles by which it was possible to make a distinction between thought and faith, philosophy and theology, but he had himself always practised them in unity and as a theologian.

The problem of the relationship between philosophy and theology is one of the problems which has always accompanied the whole development of neo-Thomism. The questions can be expressed in the following way. What is the difference between philosophy and theology as sciences? Is philosophy possible without theology or theology without philosophy? If the one science calls forth the other, what, then, is the relationship between neo-Thomist philosophy and modern philosophy? Is it possible or is it unacceptable to speak about a Christian philosophy that is different from Christian theology? If theology is thinking about faith, is faith excluded from philosophy? Can a thinker who believes (in the Christian sense) be anything else but a theologian? Can he also be a philosopher? What part, then, does faith play in his thought? If this part is essential, is he therefore not a theologian instead of a philosopher? If this part is inessential, is he therefore not expounding an artificial and abstract philosophy which lacks the ethos that has always characterized the true philosopher?

These questions have not, of course, all been asked at the same time during the course of the development of neo-Thomism, but have arisen gradually. Similarly, the neo-Thomist answers to these questions have also undergone a development. From the very beginning, however, the neo-Thomists have preserved the distinction between philosophy and theology, a distinction which has been worked out in various ways, from the one extreme of a pure 'division of labour' to the other extreme of complete separation. In the earliest days of the neo-Thomist movement, the distinction was generally viewed as a separation. Theology—or at least the acknowledged doctrine of faith—was regarded as the external norm for philosophical truth. The philosopher was guided by the accepted teaching about faith as to how he should *not* think. He was therefore able to be on his guard against errors which—since truth was one—were at the same time errors in faith and in thought.

This reasoning seldom gave scope to the inspiring influence of faith on thought. It was based on the opinion that the philosopher who, as a philosopher, did not believe explicitly, was not inwardly affected in his thought by this faith and that he thought as everyone else, either believer or unbeliever, thought. From this point of view, however, it could only cause surprise that philosophical truth, seen in this light, should remain confined to the circle of the neo-Thomists. Philosophical truth seemed to present itself differently to the Protestant and the non-Christian philosopher on the one hand and to the neo-Thomist on the other.

This surprise arose most easily with reference to certain philosophical problems. The theory of the proofs of the existence of God occupied a decisive place among these. Initially, neo-Thomism did very little but simply repeat the well-known 'five ways' from the beginning of Thomas's *Summa Theologica*. A gradual deepening of insight led to these five proofs being regarded as different explicitations of the one proof of causality—if there was something that could not explain itself, it had to be explained by something else which, in the last resort, did not need any explanation outside itself. This was consequently the First Cause or the Absolute and could only be the same as what Christianity recognized as God. But, with every successive deepening of insight, the difficulties revealed themselves more and more clearly. Kant had limited causality to the perceptible world, so that it became necessary to engage in a fundamental argument with Kant. Modern physics also put forward Kant's view of causality within the world for discussion. And the most salient difficulty was the fact that not only unbelievers, but also the vast majority of Protestant Christians continued to deny the validity of the proofs.

The whole problem of the structure of philosophical thought, if the same way of thinking was convincing for one philosopher, but not for another, thus presented itself with great insistence. Was it perhaps true to say that faith played a more essential part in philosophical thought than the neo-Thomists had initially believed? This question in turn once again raised the problem of Christian philosophy—was it meaningful to speak about a Christian philosophy at all and, if so, how could it be distinguished from a non-Christian philosophy? Neo-Thomists are still not completely in agreement about this. All that they have agreed to do is to abandon the early point of departure, namely that faith is only negatively concerned with philosophical thought. They have not, however, come to any clear conclusion concerning the positive relationship between faith and thought.

This development has brought neo-Thomism into close contact with the development of modern philosophy and with contemporary thinking as a whole. To begin with, the conviction prevailed in neo-Thomist circles that philosophical thought had reached a climax that could not be surpassed, in Thomas. This implied that neo-Thomism could only be a return to Thomas himself, that Thomas's fundamental ideas could not be given any deeper meaning, but that they could only be applied to problems which had not arisen in Thomas's own time. A further implication of this conviction was that all philosophy since Thomas was without significance. Very soon, however, neo-Thomists came to realize that quite important problems had arisen since Thomas's time and that it would be a grave and, what is more, an absolutely unthomist error to neglect the philosophical questions of the great modern philosophers. In this connection, Mercier's influence was of decisive importance.

Without realizing it, the early neo-Thomists were strongly influenced by Cartesian and post-Cartesian, especially rationalist, tendencies. Increasing contact with contemporary philosophy, however, eventually made neo-Thomists conscious of these tendencies in their thought and consequently of the need for explicit confrontation with modern philosophy. Although they were not very interested in positivism in this encounter and paid little attention to Hegelianism until quite late in the twentieth century, Mercier made them realize that they could not possibly ignore Kant. Kant's position with regard to the proofs of the existence of God was the ultimate consequence of his view of the process of knowing. The encounter between neo-Thomism and neo-Kantian criticism was therefore extremely important and proved to be the beginning of a lasting contact between neo-Thomism and the other movements in contemporary philosophy.

The question of reality was central in the philosophical movement known as criticism (see the following section). Mercier's neo-Thomism aimed to maintain an integral realism, but at the same time to acknowledge the right and even the inevitability of this central problem of criticism. Mercier went along with criticism to the point of admitting that the problem of knowledge was the true point of departure for philosophical thought and that this point of departure could only be situated in consciousness. The fact that the idea of the reality of the world was to be found in consciousness could only be explained causally from the effect of the world on consciousness. This meant that the reality of the world was deduced from consciousness.

The later neo-Thomists, such as JOSEPH MARÉCHAL (1878–

1944), were certainly no less convinced than Mercier of the need to incorporate the Kantian problem into neo-Thomist philosophy, but they criticized Mercier for having taken a wrong point of departure. They argued that, if consciousness was taken as the point of departure, it was not possible to abandon it in order to find a reality outside it. Various later neo-Thomists put forward the idea that man was, from the very beginning, in and with the outside world, with the result that realism could not be critical in the Kantian sense, as Mercier had insisted, but only immediate (LÉON NOËL, 1878–1953) or methodical (ETIENNE GILSON, b. 1884).

In the meantime, neo-Thomism came into contact not only with modern philosophy, but also with modern science. The revival of the systematic study of medieval philosophy brought the neo-Thomists into contact with the development of philology and the science of history. Contact with natural science was established more slowly and it was not until the middle of the twentieth century that a really radical exchange of views was able to take place. It was also a long time before there was any contact between neo-Thomism and biology because the theory of evolution was regarded with suspicion in Catholic circles. No change was possible here until the twentieth century, when evolution was freed from its mechanical aspect and there was no longer any need to choose between mind and matter, in other words, when mind and matter came to be regarded as closely linked.

From the very beginning, neo-Thomism has always been a metaphysical ontology. The cardinal point has always been the question of being and the neo-Thomist answer to this question has consistently pointed beyond perceptible being to the spiritual being which is revealed in thought and freedom and which ultimately leads man to acknowledge a personal God, the Creator. From this point, neo-Thomism has developed an all-embracing philosophy in which no sphere of reality, science or knowledge is ignored. In this, neo-Thomism has always, in accordance with its fundamentally metaphysical ideas, insisted on the reality of the spirit and freedom.

From the very beginning too, Leo XIII had the aim not only of promoting theology and philosophy, but also of stimulating positive science and social thinking among Catholics. Specialists in various fields were appointed to his academy and he made repeated attempts to get Catholic political and socio-economic thinking out of deadlock and to set it in motion again. In various encyclicals he defended democracy against those Catholics who tried to make a Christian principle of absolute monarchy. He put it clearly to the French Catholics that they were, as Catholics, free to strive for a restoration of the monarchy, but also that they were equally free to support the republic and that, in any case, any striving for the first should not result in harm to the life of the community as a whole. In the encyclical *Rerum Novarum* (1891), he recognized the rights of the workers in their struggle against exploitation.

Thus it is partly thanks to Leo XIII that neo-Thomism has, again from the very beginning, always been deeply concerned with social problems. Two principles have remained constant here throughout its development. The first is that the individual person should never be allowed to become so merged into the community that his dignity and freedom as an individual are sacrificed. The second is that the person should never be set over and against the community, as though the interests of the community could be sacrificed to those of one individual person. Freedom and solidarity, then, have always been defended in neo-Thomist social teaching and have always been seen as a unity. At the political level, democratic tendencies have always prevailed among neo-Thomists and have been most clearly formulated by JACQUES MARITAIN (b. 1882), who has played a leading part in neo-Thomism in connection with

D

many different problems, but whose contribution to social ethics has been his most important work.

With regard to man, questions have arisen not only in connection with freedom and social solidarity, but also in connection with his structure as soul and body. Here, neo-Thomism has followed the Thomist tradition, which elaborated the Aristotelian idea of the soul as the *form* of the body. The Cartesian view of the twofold substance was therefore rejected by the neo-Thomists, who have always insisted that neither the soul nor the body is a substance, but only the whole man. They have, however, not been able to reach agreement as to how this dual unity should be conceived. Materialism and idealism may both be rejected by this point of view, but the difficulty still remains—how should death and the immortality of the soul be conceived according to this view of the unity of man?

This brings us to the neo-Thomist problems of religious philosophy, which have, generally speaking, been dealt with by the neo-Thomists in the context of theology and relatively seldom in the context of philosophy (Maréchal, Maritain and later on Ortegat). This is, of course, closely connected also with the problem to which I have already referred, that of Christian philosophy and of establishing the dividing line between religious philosophy and theology. The problem of the immortality of the soul has, generally speaking, been dealt with philosophically, like that of the existence of God. The problem of mysticism, on the other hand, has usually been discussed theologically, but it has also occasionally been placed within the context of philosophical anthropology. In any case, the question as to how man is related to the Absolute and how the Absolute can be identified with the personal God of Christian teaching has always been of central importance to neo-Thomism.

For a long time the movement was relatively isolated. This

isolation has, however, gradually been overcome and at the moment the exchange of ideas between the neo-Thomists and other philosophers is so intensive that it is impossible to define the boundaries of the neo-Thomist school of thought. Two things keep it together—the external factor of the traditional link with certain monastic orders, universities, journals and so on, and the internal factor of a profound study of Thomas. But there is no doubt that the movement is coming closer to achieving its original aim as it tends to disappear as a school. The original intention of Leo XIII was, after all, to encourage the practice of philosophy and theology among Catholics so as to renew contact between Catholic thought and the modern world.

Despite its initial isolation, however, neo-Thomism has made an important contribution to the change in thinking that has taken place between the nineteenth and the twentieth centuries. There are many factors attributable to the influence of neo-Thomism which continue to have a powerful effect on the philosophy of our own period. Let me conclude with a summary of the main achievements of this school of thought. Nineteenth-century materialism, after careful consideration, was rejected. Freedom was defended. God, as the First Cause and Creator, was given a central place in being and a fundamental theory of being was worked out. At a later stage of its development, neo-Thomism defended the intellect while rejecting rationalism. It has striven towards a deeper understanding of man as a unity than that provided by the Cartesian idea of duality. Finally, it has sought to overcome individualism by emphasizing the need for both social solidarity and personal freedom.

2. Neo-Kantianism

I use the term neo-Kantianism or 'criticism' to denote the efforts made by philosophers to overcome the positivist thought of the nineteenth century by returning to the critical thought of Kant. These efforts began as early as the nineteenth century with thinkers like Lange, Liebmann and Riehl, who initiated a return to Kant. This return to Kant became the predominant philosophical tendency in Germany in the first quarter of the present century and also had a profound influence in the Netherlands, Italy and the Scandinavian countries. Despite the great influence of Kant in France and England, however, no neo-Kantian school was formed in either of these two countries.

There were various movements within neo-Kantian criticism itself. Some tended in the direction of realism and pragmatism, but by far the most important were the two movements which became known as the Marburg and the Baden schools. The first had its centre at the University of Marburg and the second at the Universities of Freiburg i. Br. and Heidelberg. There were considerable differences between these two schools, but, as neo-Kantianism developed, philosophers emerged who attempted to bridge the gap between them and to break through the adherence to one or other school. The leading figures of the Marburg school were HERMANN COHEN (1842–1918) and PAUL NATORP (1854–1924). The leaders of the Baden school were WILHELM WINDELBAND (1848–1915) and HEINRICH RICKERT (1863–1936).

Both schools were characterized not only by a return to Kant, but also by a common intention in returning to him. Materialism was unacceptable to these philosophers, because they were convinced that Kant had correctly demonstrated the part played by the human mind in the coming about of knowledge. For the materialists the mind was an epiphenomenon, a phenomenon that accompanied matter. For the neo-Kantians, on the other hand, an explanation of reality could only proceed from the mind. They accepted the positivists' rejection of metaphysics and this meant that it was impossible for them to return directly to Hegel.

The great problem for the criticists, then, was what part the human mind played in the process of knowing, what value had accordingly to be attributed to knowing, and what the relationship was between this knowing and an outside world. Neo-Kantianism was therefore preoccupied with the theory of knowledge, a theory which had to take into account various forms of knowledge—everyday knowledge, knowledge of the positive sciences and of philosophy, knowledge in morality and aesthetic experience, in religion and theology. Kant's distinction between pure reason, practical reason and judgement continued to guide the neo-Kantians here, but there was no question of their adhering dogmatically to Kant. Their attitude to Kant in this connection was well formulated by Windelband: 'Understanding Kant means going beyond him.'

Despite this fundamental agreement about their point of departure, the Marburg and the Baden schools differed radically from each other in certain respects. The Marburg school emphasized the logical unity of thought to such an extent that it was accused of panlogism and, despite its rejection of metaphysics, undoubtedly approached closely to Hegel. The Baden school, on the other hand, went back to the ideas of Lotze and placed central value in thought. The orientation towards logic of the neo-Kantians of the Marburg school led to their giving preference to natural science which, in addition to purely formal mathematics, they regarded as science *par excellence*. The Baden school, on the other hand, stressed the structural difference between the natural sciences and the humanities and was intent on maintaining the special character of the latter over and against the former.

The Marburg school regarded philosophy as the logical analysis of the conditions for knowing and willing. Exact natural science provided the most ideal form of knowing.

Knowledge was, for these thinkers, never a representation of reality outside knowledge itself—knowledge itself was reality. Only the legality of thought determined the coming about of knowledge. Reality itself was an entirety of logical relationships. Thought operated according to categories which were immanent in thought, so that it was *a priori* determined by these categories. Truth, the Marburg philosophers maintained, was the conformity of thought with these categories, untruth was the opposite. How such a lack of conformity was possible, however, in view of the fact that the categories were *a priori* valid, was not explained.

The will was defined purely formally, that is, by duty only by the Marburg philosophers, just as it had been by Kant. Unlike Kant, however, they did not give priority to practical reason, but to theoretical reason and, in their ethics, they were more concerned than Kant with the community. Again and again they tried to bring Kantian and Marxist ethics into harmony with each other. Like Kant, they traced religion back to ethics. They were also very interested in the science of law and endeavoured to apply their formal and logical interpretation of natural science to the science of law. On this basis, RUDOLF STAMMLER (1856–1938) and HANS KELSEN (b. 1881) developed a philosophy of law.

A peak was reached in the formalization of thought by ALBERT GÖRLAND (1869–1952) and in the attempt to harmonize Kant and Marx by KARL VORLÄNDER (1860–1928). After the death of Cohen and Natorp, the framework of the Marburg school was soon broken by ERNST CASSIRER (1874–1945) and ARTHUR LIEBERT (1878–1947), although Natorp himself had already begun the process before he died. In the last years of his life he was very open to the problems of the philosophy of life and phenomenology, and the phenomenologist Husserl was also, in turn, influenced by him in his development. Cassirer went even further in this direction and, unlike his predecessors, also devoted his attention to the humanities and developed a philosophy of man's being.

The Baden school developed differently from that of Marburg. These neo-Kantians emphasized not the logical formalization of reality, but the various forms in which reality was revealed and because of which it was, in their view, impossible to put forward one single pattern of knowing as universally valid. They made a distinction between the spheres of being, by which they understood perceptible reality, thought and values. They maintained that there was a unity of reality and thought in principle, but that thought had in fact to include reality again and again in itself. Insofar as perceptible reality was nature, this thinking of reality took place in natural science, which developed laws that were universally valid not only for nature, but also for the perceiver. The humanities, on the other hand, did not develop any universally valid laws, but described the concrete event. To be able to do this, those who practised the humanities had to have a scale of values and select what was important from the concrete reality, because it was inexhaustible. Necessarily, then, evaluation had to be a feature of the attitude of those practising the humanities towards this concrete reality, or, in other words, human reality.

The attention that the neo-Kantians of Baden gave to concrete human reality and to history has had an important influence on contemporary thought. If it is true that questions about God, man, the world and history have been central in mid-twentieth-century thinking, then the Baden school has undoubtedly made a more direct contribution to this philosophy than the Marburg school. The Baden school prepared the way for an understanding of the pluriformity of reality and made a valuable effort to understand philosophically the historicizing tendency of modern thought. These philosophers understood that no universal pattern for reality could be provided by natural science because universal legality was only one aspect of reality and not the whole of reality. That is why the philosophy of the neo-Kantians of the Baden school formed such an important contribution to the understanding of man in his concrete situation in the world and in history. The fact that the founders of the school did not always agree with the later development of thought within the school—Rickert, for example, did not understand the meaning of the philosophy of life—does not mean that they did not contribute essentially to this development. They influenced Cassirer and Liebert and, for example, HANS LEISEGANG (1890–1951) in his efforts to avoid tracing the various forms of thought back to *a priori* categories and to view them as attempts made by thought to adapt itself to a pluriform reality. BRUNO BAUCH (1877–1942) tried to bridge the gap between the two schools of Marburg and Baden by illuminating the dialectical connection between truth, value and reality. HUGO MÜNSTER-BERG (1863–1916) systematically elaborated the philosophy of values. EMIL LASK (1865–1915) devoted himself to an attempt to link the ideas of the Baden school with those of phenomeno-logy. There is, moreover, an affinity between the theory of values of this school and the way in which Max Scheler used the idea of values.

Although it has been less direct, the Marburg school has also had an influence on present-day thinking. The necessity which, so to speak, impelled the neo-Kantians of this school to reconsider Hegel meant that they prepared the way for the modern interest in this philosopher. Any attempt to outline a complete logical system was necessarily bound to lead back to Hegel, who had given it its most magnificent form. On the other hand, however, the fact that the Marburg school stressed the overwhelming importance of logic created a favourable climate for neo-positivism, in which logic also played a dominant part. The failure of the Marburg school in this attempt thus gave rise to the search for other ways of giving logic a central importance in philosophy and at the same time made thinkers aware of that aspect of reality that was opposed to logical formalization. In this way, the Marburg school indirectly contributed to the affirmation made by contemporary philosophy of the relationship between thinking and being and to the clear need to think of the concrete as concrete.

For neo-Kantian criticism, the whole of philosophy was concentrated in the theory of knowing. This was the strength of the movement, as long as the idea was accepted that knowing had to be penetrated before other spheres of thought could be entered. Any doctrine of being was rejected by neo-Kantianism as metaphysical, and ethics, aesthetics and the philosophy of religion were considered first of all in the light of the theory of knowing. The neo-Kantian emphasis on the theory of knowing meant that knowledge was primarily regarded as scientific knowledge. This accounts for the neo-Kantian tendency to identify philosophy, the theory of knowing, and the theory of science. Philosophy thus merged into a synthetic theory of the sciences. Its task was to bring out what was universal in the sciences and thus to reveal the unity of thought. This idea continued to be felt in neo-positivism.

The great strength of neo-Kantianism was lost as soon as the idea that an understanding of knowledge as the necessary point of departure for all thought began to reveal its inadequacy. In the long run, it was bound to be apparent that thought had to be practised before it could be understood—and practised in the most diverse spheres. The theory of knowing could not be given meaning until the practice of thought had been carried out and described. In addition, the priority of the theory of knowing brought neo-Kantianism very close to idealism. This tendency towards idealism, in which reality was completely merged into thought, was fully developed in the

Marburg school. It was not possible for it to be fully elaborated in the school of Baden, in which the trio, being, thought and value, played such an important part. The identification of thought and reality was at the most an ideal and not a reality for the Baden school.

The history of neo-Kantianism—its development in other countries reflected its development in Germany—was an episode in twentieth-century thought. Criticism played an essential part in philosophy in the first quarter of this century, but afterwards it declined rapidly. This decline came about not only because of the more modest place which the theory of knowing came to occupy as a result of further reflection, but also because the tendency towards idealism, which ultimately implied an absolute control of the world by thought, was unable to survive the disillusion of the reality of the twentieth century. If man controls, he is at the same time dominated. This means that he is made as much as he himself makes. This problem absorbs the twentieth century with growing intensity.

Outside Germany and the German-speaking area, neo-Kantianism had a very great influence for several decades, in the Netherlands especially. BERNARD OVINK (1862–1944), who began by following the Marburg school, gradually departed from the Marburg interpretation of Kant and developed his own original understanding of Kant's philosophy, in which the religious problem occupied a central place. ARTHUR DE SOPPER (1875–1960), who, unlike Ovink, began as a disciple of the Baden school, later developed a realistic philosophy, in which the influence of scholasticism on the one hand and that of existentialism on the other are clearly discernible. HENDRIK J. POS (1898–1955) also took neo-Kantianism as his point of departure, but was strongly influenced by phenomenology from the very beginning.

GERARD HEYMANS (1857–1930) was very much influenced by

neo-Kantianism, but dealt with it in a highly original way in an attempt to do full justice to the empiricism that occupied such a predominant place in the second half of the nineteenth century. He accepted the empirical method as the only one that could be used, even in philosophy. His thought was, however, a constant attempt to overcome empiricism precisely with the empirical method. This philosophy led him to a psychic monism, in which the psychic became the condition for and the basis of the whole empirical world. Closely connected with this philosophical train of thought was Heymans's work in the field of theoretical and empirical psychology, in which he was a pioneer in the Netherlands. Heymans's disciples continued along the same lines as Heymans himself—LEO POLAK (1880–1941) in connection with philosophy and HENRI BRUGMANS (1884–1961) in connection with psychology.

3. Neo-Hegelianism

Although there were strong tendencies towards idealism in neo-Kantianism, it was the neo-Hegelianism of the period of transition from the nineteenth to the twentieth century that presented idealism in its most pure form. After a short period of recognition in Germany, interest in Hegel's philosophy rapidly declined there. In the second half of the nineteenth century, Hegel's thought aroused attention in Italy. The initiators of the Hegelian movement were AUGUSTO VERA (1813–1885) and BERTRANDO SPAVENTA (1817–1883) and their work was continued by BENEDETTO CROCE (1866–1953) and GIOVANNI GENTILE (1875–1944). At about the same time, neo-Hegelianism was introduced into England by the book, *The Secret of Hegel* (1865), written by JAMES HUTCHISON STIRLING (1820–1909). A first generation of neo-Hegelians in England, THOMAS HILL GREEN (1836–1882), JOHN CAIRD

(1820–1898) and EDWARD CAIRD (1835–1908), developed an idealistic philosophy based on Kant and Hegel. A second generation, the leading figures in which were FRANCIS HERBERT BRADLEY (1846–1924) and BERNARD BOSANQUET (1848–1923), developed a systematic philosophy, in which Hegel's thought was given a distinctive form. It is the thought of this second generation which is of importance to us here. Neo-Hegelianism in the Netherlands, initiated by GERARD BOLLAND (1854–1922) and continued by his followers, displayed quite different aspects. The neo-Hegelian movement had little effect in Germany itself.

In order to appreciate the significance of idealism in Europe at the beginning of the present century, it is necessary to understand the inspiration of neo-Hegelianism in Italy and England. There is a characteristic distinction between these two forms of neo-Hegelianism—both were concerned with the tension between the absolute and the relative, but each was concerned with it in a different way. In the case of Bradley and Bosanquet, the tension was between individuals and the absolute. In the case of Croce and Gentile, the tension was between the historical and the absolute. This different inspiration is important because the Italian and the English neo-Hegelian movements each threw a different light on the problems of their own times.

Before this difference is discussed in greater detail, it is necessary to draw attention to what is common to both these idealistic movements. It is possible to say that, in the second half of the nineteenth century, philosophy disregarded understanding in favour of establishing. Perception had been given priority over thought, so that it could be affirmed that nothing was absolute. Neo-Hegelianism was an attempt to reverse this order of priority and to give precedence to thought rather than to perception and thus to the absolute rather than to the relative. Idealism was an attempt to understand. It did not simply establish that something was as it was, but rather attempted to appreciate why something was as it was. An insight of this kind into reality necessarily embraced the whole of reality, because every 'something' could only be completely understood in the light of totality.

Whereas the question as to how far the power of our thought reached was basic to neo-Kantianism, thought was in principle the last word as far as idealism was concerned. Thought was potentially all-embracing and philosophy was concerned only with making this potentiality present. For the idealists, reality was thought and therefore not something that was outside thought. It was therefore a question of making thought fully conscious of itself. By virtue of its being, idealism was monistic—it recognized only one reality, namely thought or the idea. The problem, however, was that this reality was not given as one. There was perception and thought, striving and willing, mind and matter. There were also many perceptions and thoughts, many aspirations and decisions and so on. There was also the perceiver and what was perceived, the thinker and what was thought, desire and what was desired, the will and what was willed. Every monism had therefore to try to demonstrate that multiplicity was appearance and unity was reality. Bradley's major work consequently bore the significant title of *Appearance and Reality* (1893).

There was always a movement from multiplicity to unity in idealism. It was thought that accomplished this movement. Thought saw through the appearance of multiplicity and discovered the reality of unity. This was, however, only possible as long as thought was in principle already at the beginning what it would be in its completion. This meant that all initial thought was a participation in absolute thought. There was therefore only completion seen from the point of view of initial thought—in itself, thought was neither completed nor uncompleted, because it was absolute. The cardinal problem for idealism was always how to reduce multiplicity to unity, because an admission of the necessity of such a reduction was an admission of multiplicity. On the other hand, anyone disregarding the need for this reduction either remained in multiplicity and was therefore not an idealist or else placed himself from the very beginning in unity, but was therefore doomed to immobility and unable to accomplish the movement of thought, because he already *was* thought. In this way, the classical dilemma of Parmenides was always returning.

The great importance of idealism at this period was the part it played in the rediscovery of the mind and freedom. Like neo-Kantianism, it discovered the mind in the world and in the practice of science. It did not, however, confine itself to the question of precisely how the mind was active in knowledge. It attempted to overcome the antithesis between knowing and what was known, so that what was known was completely absorbed in knowing. The antithesis between subject and object was valid only as a provisional antithesis. Ultimately, it was raised to a higher level and absorbed, not in the ego, but in the suprapersonal idea.

Idealism broke with the thinking of the preceding period insofar as this had been positivist and materialistic. It perpetuated this thinking insofar as it essentially shared its optimism. Therefore, what has already been said of neo-Kantianism applies *a fortiori* to idealism—it was unable to survive when the reality of the twentieth century proved to be harsher than the dreams of the nineteenth century. In England, it declined in favour of neo-realism. In Italy and France, the break was less sharp because a realistic philosophy of the spirit which was in accordance with the national philosophical tradition had developed from the idealistic train of thought.

Idealism necessarily gave rise to a movement, but this movement was either historical, as in the case of the Italian neo-Hegelians, or more 'spatial', as in the case of the English.

For Bradley, reality was, as it were, a network of relations, the threads of which the mind had to follow in order to discover the true nature of these relations. Every being was identical with the whole of relations, which it did not have, but which it *was*. This idea led to insight into the indissoluble inter-connection, in other words, the unity, of reality. There was only one reality, which revealed itself in the manifold structures of relations. This one reality was the absolute idea, which at the same time manifested itself in the subject as interiority and in the object as exteriority. There was therefore no essential difference between subject and object. This did not mean, however, that the objective aspect of reality did not display many inner contradictions. These contradictions only showed that external reality was merely appearance, since they were raised to a higher level by the subject and absorbed in the unity of the idea. On the other hand, this did not mean that the reality of the idea was a pure abstraction—it was, on the contrary, the only concrete reality. This concrete reality was at the same time universal—the idea was universal because everything was idea, but, precisely because of this, it was also concrete, since it included everything in itself.

Although Bradley and Bosanquet displayed a fundamental affinity, their philosophical attitudes were quite different. Because of his idea of relationships, Bradley, in one way or another, continued the English empirical tradition. The division between the factual and the ideal, which he felt impelled to acknowledge, remained a reality for him despite everything. He was alive to the inadequacy of the limited individual in his attempt to attain the absolute. Bosanquet, on the other hand, was from the very beginning aware of unity and had no need to search laboriously for it—he began with this unity and accepted it as the point of departure for his thought. Only the absolute was real and it was therefore the only individual reality in the strict sense of the word. Man only had reality insofar as he participated in the absolute. He had therefore to strive to transcend himself and to lose himself in the absolute. For Bosanquet as well as for Bradley, this absolute did not have a personal character—it was for both these English neo-Hegelians an impersonal divinity.

In Italian neo-Hegelianism, the movement of thought was regarded as identical with the movement of history, as was the case with Hegel himself. Yet there was here an important difference between Croce's thinking and that of Gentile. For Croce the absolute idea was itself inwardly dynamic—it was simply the total process of reality. For Gentile, on the other hand, the absolute idea was not identical with the form in which it appeared—it transcended all phenomena. Gentile's thought therefore left open the possibility of a personal God and, because of this, he was able to give a more direct impetus to the contemporary Italian philosophy of the spirit, in which the idea of a transcendental and personal God is essential. Croce was more concerned with the problems raised by the development of mankind than with the problem of being, which preoccupied Gentile. In a word, Croce was more a philosopher of civilization, Gentile more an ontologist.

Croce saw reality as the spirit which is continuously realizing itself. This self-realization takes place, in Croce's view, in a process consisting of four successive phases. In the first phase, the spirit is, in aesthetic activity, an intuition of the concrete. In the second, it is, in its logical activity, conscious of the unity of the universal and the concrete. These two phases form the theoretical sphere—the spirit that *knows* itself. The other two phases form the practical sphere—the spirit that wills itself. In the third phase, then, the spirit wills the particular, as expressed in the struggle for life, but, in the fourth phase, the spirit subordinates the particular to the universal, as happens in moral activity. But this applies equally to all human creations, and art, science, philosophy and religion are all passing aspects in the eternal process of the spirit. Only the spirit itself is eternal, but this eternity is not static, but a continuous process which is constantly renewing everything. Only the spirit is absolute.

For Gentile, on the other hand, the only reality is thought. The whole world is nothing but the self-disclosure of thought. Thought, in Gentile's view, is the divine spirit which creates the world in its self-realization. But this self-realization takes place through the medium of man who bears the divine spirit within himself. The world is therefore simply the thought of the divine spirit, insofar as this takes place through man. Everything therefore exists in the act of thought of the ego. But the ego is always more than the purely individual and subjective ego—it always transcends itself, because the divine spirit lives and works in the ego. Only this spirit, which appears in the ego, is *atto puro,* pure act—hence the name actualism for Gentile's philosophy.

Whereas neo-Kantianism was an attempt to overcome materialism by throwing light on the part played by the human mind in the process of knowing, neo-Hegelianism was not content to go no farther than the interplay between thought and the datum. It responded to the need, which was making itself more and more strongly felt, to reflect about the totality of beings and about being itself. Neo-Kantianism limited itself, at least in its initial stage, mainly to the theory of science by affirming that, in all the sciences as a whole, all that was capable of being thought was in fact thought. Idealism, on the other hand, aimed to understand all the aspects of reality, with the result that it was more energetic than the Baden school of neo-Kantian criticism in looking for the concrete. Idealism was, as it were, an abstract method of finding the concrete. The tendencies towards the concrete, totality, structure, the spirit, freedom and the absolute, which characterized the philosophical thought of the beginning of

E

the twentieth century, were all expressed in idealism. But this expression could only be provisional, because idealism not only interpreted these tendencies, but also claimed to complete them. How incomplete these aspirations were, however, was clearly demonstrated in the real development of history.

The Dutch neo-Hegelian, Gerard Bolland, attempted to overcome the positivism and empiricism of the second half of the nineteenth century and tried to show that dialectical metaphysics was bound to develop in accordance with the philosophy of Hegel. Bolland re-edited Hegel's works and provided them with a commentary as well as developing his own ideas in the spirit of Hegel in many works of his own. His philosophy tended to be an essentially practical wisdom which was concerned with the practical problems of life, mainly those of religion and politics. He rejected traditional Christianity far more vehemently than Hegel himself had done, so that he often appears to be closer to the Enlightenment than to Hegel. As in the case of the later Hegel, his attitude towards politics was authoritarian and undemocratic. In his teaching especially, he revived interest in metaphysical questions and in this way influenced not only his own students, but also the whole later development of philosophy in the Netherlands. Those who followed him applied the Hegelian dialectical method to various branches of philosophy, including the philosophy of religion, the philosophy of history and the philosophy of nature.

4. *Marxism*

Certain neo-Thomists refuse to accept the prefix 'neo-' because their intention is simply to be Thomists and to represent the teaching of Thomas and nothing else. More and more neo-Thomists, however (they now form a majority), realize that it is not possible simply to repeat a philosophy, but that it has to be thought out again in the light of the changed situation. This would seem not to be the case with Marxism. It is difficult to describe the development of Marxism—on the one hand, it takes many different forms and, on the other, it has again and again been cut across by a dogmatism that goes back directly to the letter of Marx and Engels. Partly because of this, the development of Marxism in Russia is different from its development in Western Europe, where there is a striking difference between free and 'dogmatic' Marxism. Taken as a whole, however, all Marxists reject the prefix 'neo-'. And this is quite understandable. Unlike the neo-Thomists, the neo-Kantians and the neo-Hegelians all of whom go back to a thinker whose philosophy was, for some time, relatively neglected, the modern Marxists' relationship with Marx is in an uninterrupted tradition. The prefix 'neo-' is therefore meaningless.

Contemporary Marxists keep the ideas of Marx present in the minds of modern man. The great influence exerted by Marx on contemporary thinking cannot be fully explained by the historical study of Marx—it is also a result of the presence here and now in politics and philosophy of the Marxist answer to contemporary problems. The strictly contemporary nature of this answer is often open to doubt, in view of the fact that the social, economic and political situation has changed radically since Marx's time, but then it should not be forgotten that this change has been partly brought about by Marx and Marxism and that Marx's thought goes deep enough to be still meaningful in a changed situation.

The fact that modern Marxism is so closely connected to Marx and Engels means that names are not usually important. The various schools within contemporary Marxism must, however, be briefly mentioned. Firstly, there is the philosophical school which no Marxist would recognize as Marxism, but which has been decisively influenced by Marx in its presentation of problems. This encounter between Marxism and non-Marxist philosophy is particularly prominent in France, occurring, on the one hand, in the philosophy of Merleau-Ponty, Sartre, Simone de Beauvoir and allied thinkers and, on the other, in the 'personalism' of Mounier, de Rougemont, Lacroix, Lepp and others. The former are principally concerned with the rediscovery of human freedom within Marxism, the latter with an attempt to reconcile Marxism with Christianity.

Secondly, there are the free Marxists who do not regard the teaching of Marx as dogmatic, but—in the spirit of Marx himself—as dialectical and consequently bound to develop further. This tendency is particularly prominent among socialists. The Flemish thinker, HENDRIK DE MAN, was a striking example of this school. These free Marxists are also fairly numerous in France and, in Germany, Ernst Bloch made a new and original contribution to Marxist thought.

Finally, there are the non-orthodox communists (Trotskyists) who often make use of the fact that they are not party members to further the development of Marxism, and the members of the Western communist parties who almost always follow a standard procedure of repeating the doctrines of Marx, Engels and Lenin without adding anything new to this teaching. Only a few of these thinkers have, despite their party membership, been able to preserve their freedom of thought—such men as HENRI LEFEBVRE in France, ELIO VITTORINI in Italy and, to some extent and especially in his earlier writings, the Hungarian GEORGI LUKACS.

The differences in view are, however, not very important here. It is more important to try to throw some light on the way in which Marxism provides an answer to contemporary problems. In the development of the twentieth century, there are certain aspects which confirm the Marxist in his conviction and there are others which are difficult for him to understand.

The political disruption of the present century confirms the development predicted by Marx. The fact that the proletariat has virtually ceased to exist in the West and the decreasing intensity of the class struggle that has accompanied this phenomenon are, however, in conflict with Marx's prediction.

In its view of science, Marxism is based on determinism. Economic developments and consequences are as determined as those of physics because human society is, like nature, determined. Scientific and economic developments are measured according to this standard—modern economics and physics are just as erroneous as modern philosophy. They are all expressions of the decline of the bourgeoisie and therefore dialectical announcements of the coming of proletarian society. But Marxist thinkers do not always reject modern science so uncompromisingly. Both in Russia and outside it, there is a strong tendency to accept modern physics, mainly because this has been done for a long time already by practical physicists.

If twentieth-century philosophy is to be properly understood, it is important to consider which elements of the Marxist interpretation of reality have influenced contemporary philosophy. Firstly, there is the historical and dialectical character of Marxism. Secondly, there is the essential connection that Marxism makes between philosophy and economics and politics. Thirdly, there is the way in which it conceives the relationship between the individual and society and finally the way in which it thinks of philosophy as a form of action.

For philosophy, Marx's most radical statement is perhaps: 'philosophers have simply interpreted the world differently; our task is to change it'. For the Marxist, then, philosophy has become a form of action. This idea is certainly not new—was it not the underlying idea of Plato's State?—but it is undoubtedly new and revolutionary in modern philosophy. It means that the philosopher is deeply involved in everyday reality. He no longer stands aloof from it in contemplation, but plunges into it—he is not afraid to dirty his hands in contact with it. Whether it is openly recognized or not, this idea makes itself felt everywhere in contemporary philosophy. It is effective in pragmatism, in personalism and in existentialism, where it appears in the form of 'commitment'.

Closely related to this is the intimate connection which Marxism makes between philosophy and economics and politics. If the structure of the world is, in the first place, determined by economic conditions and all civilization and all politics are dependent on these economic relationships, then philosophy is simply the reduction of this 'suprastructure' to these economic relationships. However firmly contemporary philosophy may be opposed to a materialism that reduces everything to economics, it is nonetheless true that the close connection between economics and all the phenomena of society and 'civilization', including philosophy, is recognized today. A philosophy that has moved away from reality is to some extent still put to the test in idealism, but it has reached deadlock over the concept that thought is concerned with the concrete reality, that this reality is first and foremost a reality of human relationships and that these may not be exclusively or even primarily determined by economics, but are certainly partly determined by economic conditions.

Nineteenth-century materialism may be unacceptable to us today, but the continued defence of materialism by modern Marxism keeps us alive to the fact of our being in this concrete, material world, and prevents twentieth-century philosophy from losing itself in abstract reflections. Even though modern philosophy may reject the Marxist view of the relationship between the economic infrastructure and the social suprastructure, Marxism does keep us alive to the idea that the mind does not exist without matter and that the mind can only be analysed by examining the way in which it reveals itself in matter and creates its form in the various patterns of civilization from matter.

Marxism is therefore essentially also a philosophy of the human community. The fact that modern philosophy is so intensely preoccupied with the community is undoubtedly attributable to the shocks that have disturbed Western society during the present century and which still continue to affect the whole world. But present-day thinking about this development is also partly determined by Marxism, which offers us a concrete philosophy of the human community in which we are obliged to take sides. As Lenin once said, 'those without a party are just as hopeless bunglers in philosophy as they are in politics'. Marxism brought the problem of the relationship between the individual person and the community to a head with its philosophy of the community. Contemporary philosophy refuses to accept both the Marxist subordination of the individual person to the community and the liberalist subjection of the community to the individual. But it is not content simply to reject these two views—its aim is to rediscover the relationship between the individual and the community at a higher level. This is the problem which confronts not only personalism, but also neo-Thomism, the philosophy of life, the philosophy of the spirit and existentialism.

Marx had a dynamic, not a static, view of society—he saw society as constantly developing and his task as the provision of a prognosis of this development. If philosophy is action, then this prognosis has to be built up, in the case of Marxism, on the existing situation which philosophy has to change. If Marxist materialism does not mean that everything is matter, as the Marxists of the school of Moleschott and Büchner maintain, but that society is built up on material, that is, economic relationships, then this materialism can be historical and dialectical. It is historical because it changes with history and influences history. It is dialectical because it is always within a dialectical process—the tensions between nature and human society and between capitalism and the proletariat determine the movement of the process of history.

Marx strengthened and intensified the historical element that is a prominent feature both of twentieth-century and of nineteenth-century philosophy and it is partly thanks to him that all contemporary forms of philosophy are, in a certain sense, philosophies of history. In this, the philosophy of history is at the same time always social philosophy, not only because Marx emphasized the Christian idea of the unity of mankind, but also because he stressed that all personal and social action is firmly rooted in class. Unfortunately, Marxism tends to regard this class basis of all individual and communal activity as the only basis and to give it an absolute value, thus enabling modern Marxists lightly to dismiss everything that is not communist as bourgeois and decadent. This has resulted in Marxism cutting itself off from the development of modern thought and in Marx's dialectics becoming an inflexible and mechanical means of reasoning.

Similarly, the Marxist insistence on the connection between philosophy and politics is also its strength and its weakness. Marx succeeded in gripping the nineteenth-century working classes not only by his attempts to improve their conditions, but also by providing them with a total view of life which was worth working and even dying for. Politics alone cannot do this. If Marxist politics are in fact able to do this, it is because these politics are only one side of the coin, the other side being a philosophy which provides a complete view of life and the world. On the other hand, however, this connection between philosophy and politics has a paralysing effect as soon as the politics have become a real power. Power can only be maintained by a firm political line and an intolerance of any deviation from this policy. Thus, as soon as political power becomes a reality, the philosopher is bound to lose his freedom and therefore will be unable to practise authentic philosophy.

In a sense, Marxism is here paying the penalty of Marx's idealistic background. The idea that politics and philosophy, the concrete and the abstract, are one is, after all, derived from idealism. This postulated unity of politics and philosophy does away both with the freedom of politics, which must fit into the scheme, and with the freedom of thought, which must not contradict the political line. This has led to the constant contradictions in Marxism—the only possible way of overcoming these would be by seeing Marxism in its fortuitous concreteness, in other words, as the answer at a given time to the existing situation, an answer which was bound to develop as the situation itself developed and which can only develop in freedom. One of the most fascinating aspects of twentieth-century Marxism is its continued attempts to revitalize its rigid dialectics.

3 Answers from the Change of Direction

No philosopher is completely isolated from the past and no philosopher gives form to his ideas without a knowledge of the history of philosophy. This applies even to Descartes, despite his own rejection of links with the past. In calling the answers given in this chapter new, then, I do not mean that they are completely independent of philosophical tradition, but that they do not go back directly to an earlier philosopher, whose principles form the basis of the later philosophy. Newness in philosophy is always relative. No new question and no new answer is completely isolated from the past. No earlier question and no earlier answer is entirely without contemporary value if they are really philosophical questions and answers.

There is, then, no unbridgeable gulf between the philosophical problems dealt with in this chapter and those dealt with in the previous chapter. In both cases, answers are given to the same problems and the different philosophies all stem from the same past. The difference is one of emphasis, with regard both to the present problems and to the philosophical past. Thus, the problems dealt with here have influenced those dealt with in the previous chapter as much as those discussed in the previous chapter have influenced those treated here. Contemporary thought is characterized by a living contact between different philosophical movements. This contact sometimes results in a certain eclecticism, but it also frequently leads to a very fruitful broadening and deepening of original points of view.

In this chapter, it is necessary to indicate the various ways in which those philosophers who are not tied to tradition have replied to the problems that arose at the turn of the century. Every real philosopher, of course, gives his own answer. All classification into philosophical movements is therefore to some extent bound to be arbitrary. Certain philosophers are grouped together because they ask similar questions and provide similar answers. But this similarity is never a complete identity—the dividing lines are always fluid and one philosopher may have many points in common with two other philosophers who are very different from each other. But, because a discussion of each of the leading thinkers in isolation from the rest might well lead to a piecemeal treatment which would conceal the great movements in contemporary thought, I have attempted to group philosophers together in such a way that the fundamental questions and answers of today are revealed as clearly as possible.

1. *Pragmatism*

Although it is possible to point to allied schools of thought in Europe and in England, pragmatism is essentially an American philosophy. The New World believed that it had found its own mode of thought in pragmatism. In Europe, on the other hand, pragmatism had a certain following, but only for a time. But it was one of the answers given to the problems posed at the beginning of the present century and, because this answer had a deep influence in Europe on the questions raised by very divergent tendencies of thought, it cannot be left out of this survey of twentieth-century philosophy. After CHARLES S. PEIRCE (1839–1914) had prepared the way, pragmatism was fully developed by WILLIAM JAMES

(1842–1910) and JOHN DEWEY (1859–1952). I shall deal here principally with James who was, without any doubt, the philosopher who exerted the greatest influence on European thought during the first quarter of this century.

At the suggestion of Peirce, James called his philosophy pragmatism, but he also used the terms radical empiricism and pluralism and an account of James's philosophy can usefully begin with a consideration of these three terms. Firstly, why did he call his thought empiricism, and what is more, radical empiricism? An answer to this question will enable us to understand his pluralism more easily and this will in turn lead us to an understanding of pragmatism as the central element in James's philosophy. This is not, however, a 'historical' sequence. The books which give rise to these names appeared in the reverse order—*Pragmatism* appeared in 1907, *A Pluralistic Universe* in 1909 and *Essays in Radical Empiricism* in 1912. But James's earlier writings are more easily understood in the light of his later writings, because his later ideas provide the latent motivation for his other ideas. Furthermore, he did in fact use the term 'radical empiricism' at a very early stage of his development.

James regarded his own thought as an extension of English empiricism, but his empiricism was not an attempt to build up reality from isolated facts or perceptions. James himself explained the radical nature of his empiricism in the following way: 'To be radical, an empiricism must neither admit into its constructions any element that is not directly experienced, nor exclude from them any element that is directly experienced. For such a philosophy, *the relations that connect experiences must themselves be experienced relations, and any kind of relation experienced must be accounted as 'real' as anything else in the system.*'[1] Traditional empiricism had little concern for these

[1]*Essays in Radical Empiricism*, London 1912, 42 (author's italics).

relations, certainly for the connecting relations. Rationalism, on the other hand, James claimed (and he had Hegel in mind here) 'tends to emphasize universals and to make wholes prior to parts in the order of logic as well as in that of being. Empiricism, on the contrary, lays the explanatory stress upon the part, the element, the individual, and treats the whole as a collection and the universal as an abstraction.'[2]

What part does consciousness play in James's philosophy? Consciousness, he says, does not exist. With this, he does not imply materialism. 'I mean only to deny,' he says, 'that the word stands for an entity, but to insist most emphatically that it does stand for a function.'[3]

There is not a being of material things and, alongside this, a matter of which our thoughts are made. Thoughts fulfil a function in experience, the function of knowledge. There is only one matter and that is experience. Knowledge is a special manner in which experiences come into contact with each other. *Experience, I believe, has no such inner duplicity; and the separation of it into consciousness and content comes, not by way of subtraction, but by way of addition.*[4] '*That entity* [of the consciousness] *is fictitious, while thoughts in the concrete . . . are made of the same stuff* [that is, of experience] *as things are.*'[5]

James distinguishes two forms of knowledge—'knowledge of acquaintance' and 'knowledge about'. The first is the direct knowledge of perception, the second is the indirect knowledge of the concept. In a certain sense, both are experience, but the first, knowledge of acquaintance, takes precedence. James regarded concepts not so much as the result of perception, but rather as a means of coming to new perceptions. The concept was, in his view, at the service of perception. A real enrichment

[2]*Ibid.*, 41.
[3]*Op. cit.*, 3.
[4]*Op. cit.*, 9 (author's italics).
[5]*Op. cit.*, 37 (author's italics).

of knowledge and thus a real increase of human possibilities could only come from perception. But, in reducing both material things and human ideas to experience, was James not in fact suggesting a form of monism, in which the whole of reality was nothing more than experience?

James did not see it in this light. He did acknowledge two ideas, both of which can easily lead and have in fact often led to monism—the pantheistic idea of God and the idea of evolution. Together with Hegel (absolutism), James believed that the philosophy of the absolute agreed with the pluralistic philosophy 'in that both identify human substance with divine substance'.[6] Absolutism, however, thinks in what James called the 'all-form', believing that everything that is can be comprehended at once. Radical empiricism, on the other hand, thinks in the 'each-form'—human knowledge is never complete. The new is always presenting itself, hence the idea of 'pluralism'. We live in a reality that is never closed, but always developing.

This is possible because time is essential to this reality— without time, there is no development, no history and no freedom. The unity of things is not given to us in the all-form of experience, but in the unceasing stream of our experiences. Every experience is an experience in the each-form and adds something new to what has gone before, though not as a thing that is added to another thing, in which case we fall into 'the difficulty of seeing how states of consciousness can compound themselves'.[7] But states of consciousness are no more things than consciousness itself is a thing. They are not tangible— there is only the stream of experience, in which everything runs into and interpenetrates everything else. 'Sensational experiences *are* their "own others", then, both internally and externally. Inwardly they are one with their part, and out-

[6]*A Pluralistic Universe,* London 1909, 34.
[7]*Op. cit.,* 281.

wardly they pass continuously into their next neighbours.'[8]
Reality is a living stream, from which only concepts cut static
unities. To see a direct reflection of reality in concepts
(intellectualism) is to mutilate this reality completely.

Concepts are a means of coming to new experiences. Every
theory is valuable insofar as it is capable of leading us to new
experiences. Truth and value are the same—they are to be
found in the possibility of verification by future experiences.
'*True ideas are those that we can assimilate, validate, corroborate
and verify. False ideas are those that we can not* . . . The truth of an
idea is not a stagnant property inherent in it. Truth *happens*
to an idea. It *becomes* true, is *made* true by events. Its verity *is*
in fact an event, a process; the process namely of its verifying
itself, its veri-*fication*. Its validity is the process of its valid-
ation.'[9]

Concepts, judgements or theories are true if they appear to be
manageable in practice, in other words, if they are effective.
An idea that is not effective is a false idea. Truth is a quality of
concept, judgement, reasoning or theory, not of things
themselves. They are not only true if they demonstrate their
significance for material existence, but also if they are effective
in the spheres of science, art or religion. Although the world
is undoubtedly real, this reality is nowhere firmly established.
It consists of many separate beings which are continuously
moving and developing. James was convinced of the spiritualistic character of this reality. Man is placed in this constantly
renewing reality with a free will. 'Free will means novelty,
the grafting on to the past of something not involved therein.'[10]

James referred to his pragmatism as a new name for various
old ways of thinking. As a result of studying for years in

[8]*Op. cit.,* 285.
[9]*Pragmatism. A New Name for Some Old Ways of Thinking,* New York
and London 1928, 201 (author's italics).
[10]*Op. cit.,* 117.

Europe, he came to know European philosophy as few Americans have ever known it. At the same time, however, he also came to realize that a new path had to be followed. In this, his underlying inspiration was clearly developing American life—life with its gaze directed to the future rather than to the past, a way of life more orientated towards action than towards reflection. He also took over several fundamental ideas from Peirce. We must now consider James's position with regard to the problems posed at the turn of the century.

James looked for the new and, in this, he acknowledged his affinity with Bergson. In his conviction that the world was evolving, he showed the nineteenth-century idea of evolution, and he shared, too, the same century's idea of progress. But it was also precisely here that he differed from the nineteenth century—by establishing a connection between progress, newness and free will. James was convinced that determinism precluded renewal, whereas freedom made it possible: 'free will is thus a general cosmological theory of *promise*'.[11] Freedom was therefore, for James, a 'belief' in the sense in which Hume used the word, a conviction which could not be proved empirically, but which had motivating power.

With pragmatism, James also established a close link between thought and action. He himself acknowledged his affinity in this on the one hand with Dewey and Schiller and, on the other, with Blondel and Le Roy. He insisted that thought was a form of action and that, since action was directed towards effect, towards reaching something, thought was worth what it reached. Its value could therefore only be verified empirically against what it reached. This is clearly an application of the pragmatic principle of verification, in which James anticipated the use of this principle in neo-positivism on the one hand and the interpretation of natural science as a

[11]*Op. cit.*, 119.

F

mode of action on the other. At the same time, he also anticipated the struggle for determinism in physics: 'The general
"uniformity of nature" is presupposed by every lesser law.
But nature may be only approximately uniform.'[12]

With empiricism, James not only continued the nineteenth-
century tradition, but also transformed it in such a way as to
make it acceptable to the twentieth century. His radical
empiricism was not a continued atomization of experience,
but rather an appeal to real experience which displays a
structure. It contains elements which bring James very near to
the *Gestalt* psychologists on the one hand and to phenomenology on the other, although it contains nothing of Husserl's
intuitive glimpse of the essence, because everything is directed
towards action. It even includes a vague definition of Heidegger's real and unreal being: 'Free will pragmatically means
novelties in the world, the right to expect that in its deepest
elements as well as in its surface phenomena, the future may
not identically repeat and imitate the past. That imitation *en
masse* is there, who can deny it?'[13]

In this, James was referring both to human and to sub-
human nature. In the last resort, progress was possible only if
there was free will. The idea of free will 'holds up improvement as at least possible; whereas determinism assures us that
our whole notion of possibility is born of human ignorance,
and that necessity and impossibility between them rule the
destinies of the world'.[14] By linking freedom, possibility and
human future together in this way, James prepared the way for
certain ideas which were later to be more fully developed by
the existential philosophers. As in the case of existentialism,
there was, in James's case too, a close relation between freedom
and time.

[12] *Op. cit.,* 119.
[13] *Op. cit.,* 118-9.
[14] *Op. cit.,* 119.

James's attitude towards metaphysics was ambivalent. He did not reject it, but judged it pragmatically according to its possibilities for action. On the other hand, however, his theory of experience developed into a metaphysics which, unlike his pluralism, came very close to monism. This monism of experience was in fact James's answer to the problem of idealism. Not everything is thought, but everything is experience. Thus he made what dominated philosophy in the nineteenth century as implicit metaphysics explicitly metaphysical.

James influenced European thought in many of its forms, including existential philosophy, neo-realism and neo-positivism. It is not possible to discuss the thought of the other two leading American pragmatists, Dewey and Peirce, here, although we are at present becoming more and more aware of the extent to which James was influenced by Peirce. It is, moreover, not really necessary to analyse Peirce's philosophy, since it is only in recent years that he has been rediscovered and, in the course of this still incomplete process, what is coming to light is that many contemporary philosophical ideas, especially those of neo-positivism, were already present in Peirce. But, so far at least, Peirce has not directly influenced European philosophy—he has only had an indirect influence, via James and Dewey. This, however, appears to be changing now and any future survey of twentieth-century thought will probably have to take this into account.

2. The Criticism of Science

If the development of European philosophy is to be properly understood, it is most important not to lose sight of the great strength of the various national traditions. The French philosopher has grown up with Montaigne, Pascal and above all with Descartes; the English philosopher with Locke, Berkeley and above all with Hume; and the German philosopher has grown up with Kant. This does not, of course, mean that there is no international exchange of ideas—the English, French and German philosophers that I have mentioned are influential everywhere. But, in order to gain an impression of the great strength of national tradition in philosophy, it is instructive to compare, for example, the criticism of Renouvier in France with the criticism of the neo-Kantians in Germany, or the idealism of Hamelin in France with that of the neo-Hegelians in England, or neo-realism in England with neo-positivism in Germany and Austria. Philosophy transcends national frontiers, not by ignoring them, but by including them—this was clear in the case of James's pragmatism.

It is therefore not without good reason that we tend to use the term 'criticism of science' almost exclusively for French speculation about science, although all contemporary philosophy is critical in its consideration of science. But there is a tradition in this French theory of science which gives it a character entirely of its own. It was given form in France in the work of the philosopher EMILE BOUTROUX (1845–1921) and the mathematician HENRI POINCARÉ (1854–1912) and further developed by the physicist PIERRE DUHEM (1861–1916) and the philosopher EMILE MEYERSON (1859–1933). The criticism of science also played an important part in the work of EDOUARD LE ROY (1870–1954). In the case of all these thinkers, it is in the tradition of French spiritualism. This tradition was also continued in the work of LÉON BRUNSCHVICG (1869–1944), GASTON BACHELARD (1884–1962) and FERDINAND GONSETH (born 1890). Here, I shall first try to outline very briefly the thought of these three philosophers and then examine the nature of their answer to the dominant problems of this century.

Brunschvicg had a very great influence on French thought in the period between the two world wars. He strove to find a coherent explanation of the great problems of life in the light of the phenomenon of science, a striving that has been termed scientism. In this respect, he continued the traditions of the nineteenth century and, in particular, the tradition of Comte. Yet, despite his intense striving towards unity, Brunschvicg displayed a great inner disunity. He attempted to consider the problem of positivism in an idealistic way. This impressive attempt to synthesize positivism and idealism is reflected in his major work, *Le Progrès de la Conscience dans la Philosophie Occidentale* (1927). Another side of Brunschvicg can be seen in the man who edited the works of Pascal and wrote in a masterly manner about Montaigne and Pascal—the philosopher of the religious existential problem. But this aspect of Brunschvicg's work never succeeded in penetrating his synthesis of positivism and idealism. It remained, as it were, alongside it, unreconciled, an aspect of his own being, something he did not know what to do with, but which his own inner conviction and honesty prevented him from concealing.

The great struggle of our own times is therefore clearly expressed in Brunschvicg, in whose thought the three different philosophies of positivism, idealism and existentialism occur. What is, however, common to all these three tendencies is historization. Consciousness is not suddenly present—it comes about in history and finds realization in science. Individual human consciousness is a process of man's gradually making the historical consciousness of mankind his own. The spirit is not directed towards objects—it produces them. Philosophy is nothing but a bringing to consciousness of the creative activity of the spirit in the history of mankind. This is most clearly observed in the process of the exact sciences. Concepts and theories are not representations of a reality that transcends the spirit, but actions of the spirit, by means of which truth comes about. Thus the human spirit comes to a knowledge of itself. There is nothing that transcends the spirit of man.

Brunschvicg's humanism is therefore a humanism of the spirit of man which cannot acknowledge any goodness above or outside itself.

Whereas Brunschvicg did not attempt to incorporate the existential problem into his synthetic thought and interpreted development, unlike Bergson, rationalistically and idealistically, Bachelard's way of thinking was more powerfully influenced by Bergson. As with Brunschvicg, there is a powerful tension in Bachelard's thought, but he did not try to exclude the existential problem from his philosophy—on the contrary, he tried to include it within the framework of the criticism of science. Like Brunschvicg and Gonseth, and Boutroux and Meyerson before them, Bachelard did not simply remain content with presenting a theory of science. Rather, he took the criticism of science as his point of departure for an attempt to understand man's being.

Bachelard's thought may be briefly summarized as follows. The philosophy of the sciences has to learn to take into account one of the most characteristic features of modern science—the continuous transformation of experimental values into rational values and of rational values into experimental values, the constant interaction of the *a priori* and the *a posteriori*. In science, there is no question of choosing between an empiricist or a rationalist point of view. Empiricism and rationalism are indissolubly united. The empiricism of the facts has to be understood and the rationalism of the principles has to be applied. There is no fact without theory and no theory without fact. The theory of science can only develop in a dialectical manner in the constant interaction of the rational and the empirical aspects. For this reason, the philosophy of the sciences—and therefore all philosophy—is of necessity open in its structure. It is never closed, but constantly developing, like reality itself.

This throws light on the nature of the human spirit which

is seen as neither without structure, nor as established once and for all time. It is constantly developing. For this reason, all scientific and philosophical thought is always provisional—every phase prepares the way for a new phase. This should not give rise to distrust in thought, since it is precisely because of this development that thought remains adapted to the constantly developing spirit. One of the most important tasks of the philosophy of the sciences is that of fathoming the structure of thought in its relationship to reality in the concrete. In so doing, the criticism of science is practising a psychology which is essentially a metaphysics of the relationship between the human spirit and reality.

The Swiss philosopher Gonseth was initially very close to neo-positivism, but gradually came nearer to the tradition of the French criticism of science. He did not regard philosophy as a rational system *a priori*, but as a way of thinking which always had to remain open to experience, both universal human experience and scientific experience. The facts force theory to be revised and extended, but, on the other hand, theory opens the way to the recognition of new facts. This dialectical aspect, which is so prominent in modern science, cannot be excluded from philosophy. For this reason, the leading ideas of philosophy must always be provisional ideas, always open to change and possible rejection.

Universal human experience is not independent of scientific experience. Methodology and the theory of knowledge of the sciences thus form a central point in philosophical thought. In its development, science is again and again confronted with crises and these crises determine its progress. This applies equally to philosophy, which reflects about man's situation in the world. Philosophy cannot avoid the state of crisis, and has even to bring it about in order to be truly philosophy. This thinking about man is of necessity always open. It is not relativism, since it is orientated towards progression in truth.

To a far greater extent than some German and English tendencies in philosophy, this French criticism of science always held the view that science is an affair of man and that any attempt to understand science must also lead to an understanding of man. Conversely, any theory of science also presupposes an integral speculation about man and his world and, ultimately, about being.

The element of development also emerged more and more clearly in this French theory of science. In this, the movement continued the tradition of the nineteenth century. It was historical, just as the philosophies of Hegel and Comte were historical—Brunschvicg's philosophy was, after all, an attempt to combine the idealistic historical thought of Hegel and the positivistic historical thought of Comte. Were Hegel and Comte not closer to each other than we have so far been inclined to think? Is it simply a coincidence that both insisted that ideas dominate the world?

In the case of Bachelard and Gonseth, the idealistic aspect of Hegel's thought was not stressed and indeed almost disappeared, whereas the dialectical aspect of his philosophy, whether or not through the medium of Marx, was strongly emphasized. All these philosophers of the criticism of science are thus characteristic of our own times in stressing the relativity of thought, but in rejecting relativism. Historical development itself contains a necessary element. This is, of course, Hegelian, but, in the case of the French critics of science, the necessary element remains an aspect alongside the other element of empirical coincidence. It is never possible to say *a priori* what experience will provide. All that can be said is that experience can only speak to us in a theory. Experiences are often explained by a theory which does not really permit such an explanation. But this only becomes apparent when a new theory is discovered into which the experiences fit.

This unrest of the present age is clearly expressed in the work of Bachelard and Gonseth. Brunschvicg, on the other hand, reflects the prevalent mood of the previous generation, that of the certainty of development. Bachelard and Gonseth are aware that the certainty of this development is closely linked to human freedom—hence their emphasis on openness, which man is also able to refuse, thus setting the seal on his own downfall. As with James, the fact is for none of these philosophers a separate atom, but something that is within the structure of its theory. This theory is, in turn, within the structure of the basic philosophical ideas and these are, in turn, within the structure of the manner in which man interprets his own being.

This constantly renewed insight into man as a being who interprets himself is a deepening of the historicism of the nineteenth century which we of the twentieth century owe to Wilhelm Dilthey. It is an insight which occurs again and again, not only in the criticism of science, but also in personalism and existentialism. To a very great extent, modern psychology and sociology derive their strength from this basic idea, as do phenomenology in its later development and neo-realism in England. The need to see reality as structured is felt everywhere. As Hegel argued, the one is always, to some extent, the other. Knowledge of science implies knowledge of man, knowledge of man implies knowledge of the world and knowledge of the world in turn implies knowledge of science. But this is not a closed circle. The relationship between man, the world and science is always open in a developing relativity, which is either seen as absolute itself or else placed in relation to a transcendent Absolute.

3. *Historicism*

Historicism is a typical feature of nineteenth-century thought which has been not rejected, but changed by our century, in that the polarity of genesis and structure has been given a central position. It has continued to have an effect in almost every contemporary philosophical tendency, the only possible exceptions being a few movements at the beginning of the twentieth century. These include English idealism and early neo-realism, the neo-positivism of the 'Viennese circle', early neo-Thomism and early phenomenology. But, of these, English idealism and orthodox neo-positivism have disappeared, neo-realism and neo-Thomism have discovered historicity and, in his later thought, Husserl had to give his attention to the historical problem. It would seem as though philosophers had first to see the structure of reality over and against its genesis, giving their exclusive attention to this, before coming to the idea of the unity of genesis and structure.

If twentieth-century historicism owes its existence to one man in particular, then it is certainly to the nineteenth-century thinker, WILHELM DILTHEY (1833–1911) to whom we can attribute the creation of the modern historical idea. Dilthey was not only concerned with philosophy, for his interest extended equally to philology, literature, history, psychology and sociology. His essentially historical view, which broke with the thought of the nineteenth century and played a decisive part in forming the vision of our own times, was served by an all-embracing knowledge. Many twentieth-century philosophers were deeply influenced by Dilthey, including EDUARD SPRANGER (b. 1882), THEODOR LITT (1880–1962), HANS LEGISEANG (1890–1951), ERNST TROELTSCH (1856–1923) and OSWALD SPENGLER (1880–1936), but most of these thinkers could also be named in connection with other philosophical movements. Yet those named in different contexts must also be named here. This applies above all to Germany. The neo-Kantianism of the Baden school was considerably influenced by Dilthey, but, even after the decline of neo-

Kantianism, German philosophy would be quite unthinkable without Dilthey.

But, although this applies especially to German philosophy in the present century, it also applies to the whole of European thought. During the first quarter of the twentieth century, there were very few philosophers in the rest of Europe who reacted against late nineteenth-century thinking by adopting an anti-historical attitude or by developing an ontology which accorded little or no place to historicity. The latter tendency may perhaps be found in Lavelle's thought and the neo-realists of our own period display a certain anti-historical tendency, but, generally speaking, both French and English philosophers have been, in this century, as much involved in the struggle with history as their German counterparts. The aim in this struggle has been to achieve a synthesis between the historicism of the nineteenth century and the 'structuralism' of the early part of this century. All the philosophers who have been involved in this struggle have thus followed the same path on which Dilthey first set out, whether they were acquainted with his work or not.

Does this return to the historical idea mean that twentieth-century philosophers are completely preoccupied with the history of philosophy, as was, to a very great extent, the case in the previous period? Certainly not. All that it means is that philosophers have now become acutely aware of the fact that thought itself develops, that it *is* historical, both in the individual thinker and in the history of mankind. The terms, concepts, ideas, modes of thought and theories that are used by the philosopher, the theologian or the scientist are historically determined. They do not have the absolute character of being necessarily what they are and incapable of being otherwise. The reality which the philosopher encounters and which he takes as the starting-point for his thought is also historically determined and can only be understood as a developing reality. The mood in which thought moves is a historical mood and the manner in which man understands himself is dependent on the history of his understanding of himself.

This tendency was, to some extent, also present even fifty or so years before Dilthey, in the thought of Hegel and Comte, but, in both cases (even in that of Comte!) the insight was contained within a metaphysical structure which contemporary philosophers are not inclined to accept, because necessity is given too great a priority in this structure over the accidental. Modern philosophy does not reject the idea of necessity in history, but it is anxious to recognize its accidental aspect. The problem with which philosophy is struggling now is that of the intimate bond linking the necessary and the accidental. It is a question of recognizing their unity—the necessity of the accidental and the accidental character of necessity.

It was Dilthey who made this possible and his thought is still, in a sense, so exemplary that the ideas of this nineteenth-century philosopher in fact throw the best light on the historical thinking of our own times. Dilthey understood that history is first and foremost the history of the manner in which man experiences and interprets the world. This means that history is the development of man's being. This development is not, however, the simple history which causally deduces an event from a preceding event. It is the development of man's interpretation of himself and there are various possible structures within which this can take place. Philosophy has to learn how to *understand* these structures.

For Dilthey, this 'understanding' is of fundamental importance. In the first place, it plays a part in the psychology of the individual. I still do not understand the other person when I can explain why action B had to come about causally as the consequence of action A. It is also necessary to make clear what meaning 'causal' has in this context. Concepts which can validly be used for the material reality cannot be applied unchanged to the human reality. But, apart from this, the causal explanation, however it may be understood, still remains an explanation from without. The other person remains a stranger to me, a thing, albeit a human thing.

Understanding, which is quite different from causal *explanation*, is only possible through identification. Whoever wishes to understand the other person must try to identify himself with him. What is more, the extent to which he understands him depends on the extent to which his attempt at identification succeeds. In addition to an *explanatory* psychology—and Dilthey did not dispute that there is a strong case for this—there must also be an *understanding* psychology, if the psychologist wishes to find man really as man. If explanatory psychology maintains that action B is the consequence of action A and, as a result, also places it *after* action A, understanding psychology similarly encounters the question of time, but as something qualitatively different from the divisible time of physically explanatory psychology. It is the qualitatively dynamic time of man's interpretation of himself.

If man's interpretation of himself is constantly in movement and can only be grasped in understanding, this is of the greatest significance both for our ordinary knowledge of men and for scientific psychology. But the significance of this idea extends even further—it is only in this way that we can really grasp the meaning of what the creative prose writer or poet has to say to us. His work is the expression of a temporally dynamic interpretation of himself, the flexible structure of which has to be grasped in understanding. The work of art too can be explained on the basis of dependence, derivation and so on, but all explanation of a work of art remains external and, left to itself, it has the effect of killing the work as a work of art. What is essential here is to understand the meaning of the work of art by an interpretation of the artist or writer himself.

The same also applies to philosophy. A philosopher's thought is always determined by a background to which the philosopher does not consciously revert. This background may have different structures. The different forms of philosophical thought can therefore be classified according to the structure that underlies them. Since the structure forms the background to thought and is therefore pre-philosophical, it must also be rediscovered in non-philosophers, in theologians and artists, writers and scientists, in other words, in every man.

Dilthey thus distinguished three basic structures—the structure of the man of intellect, that of the man of feeling and that of the man of will. The man of intellect forms a materialistic or positivistic view of the world for himself, the man of feeling a pantheistic view, as in German idealism, and the man of will a view of life that is based on the idea of freedom, as revealed in the case of Plato, in Christianity and in Kant. These structures can only be brought to life by understanding. The philosopher's task in this understanding is to keep as open a mind as possible and also to try to understand those structures which are not his own. Of course there are many variations of these different forms of man's view of the world and of life, dependent on the historical situation and the individual character of the thinker himself.

Dilthey did genuinely pioneering work in establishing the relationship between genesis and structure. In his historicism, he strove towards their unity and his philosophy did in principle mark the end of the atomistic view of history and reality. Side by side with his historicism was his idea of the individual's solidarity with the community that bears him up. This idea prepared the way for social psychology and the sociology of the sciences, as practised later by Scheler among others. Dilthey viewed all this against the background of human freedom, which is determined neither by necessity nor by the accidental and can therefore only be exercised in understanding. Thus the twentieth century was already present in Dilthey—this explains why men of his own time paid little or no attention to what he had to say and why contemporary man is coming more and more to realize how deeply he is influenced by Dilthey's thought.

4. *Irrationalism*

The word 'irrationalism' is used in three senses. Firstly, it can be used to denote the conviction that reality is unfathomable and that this can be demonstrated by reason (*ratio*). Secondly, it can mean the conviction that reality is not only unfathomable, but also contradictory and absurd in itself and that, once again, this can be shown by reason. Finally, it can be applied to the conviction that reason itself is unreliable and distorts reality. It is preferable not to use the term irrationalism in the first case, since it would then be necessary to call all the great philosophers—for example, Plato, Plotinus, Augustine, Thomas Aquinas, Nicholas of Cusa, Pascal, Kant and Heidegger —irrationalists. The term may, however, be used in the second case and applied perhaps to such a philosopher as Kierkegaard. It is only in the third case that the term is completely appropriate. The question remains, however, as to whether the second and the third cases can be separated, for can there be an inner contradiction of reality, without reason sharing in it?

Here, however, it is above all a question of the inner contradiction of reason itself. There is necessarily a contradiction here, but this is not a refutation, but a confirmation of irrationalism. The irrationality of reality must of necessity be expressed in the irrationality of reason. What is a refutation of irrationalism for the man who believes in reason is a confirmation for the irrationalist. The irrationalist can devise a rational system in order to demonstrate the absurdity of reason. This was perhaps carried to its furthest extreme in contemporary philosophy by LUDWIG KLAGES (1872–1956). Similar ideas were put forward in the sphere of history by THEODOR LESSING (1872–1933), the title of whose book, *Geschichte als Sinnegebung des Sinnlosen* (1916)—*History as the Interpretation of Meaninglessness*—is very characteristic of his thought. Irrationalistic tendencies coincide in Lessing's thought with Dilthey's historicism and this also applies to some extent to the thought of OSWALD SPENGLER (1880–1936), as reflected especially in his work, *Der Untergang des Abendlandes* (1918–22).

As a reaction, irrationalism is deeply rooted in Western philosophy. The point of departure is Descartes's antithesis between soul and body. As far as science is concerned, this antithesis led to the opposition between the meaningful theory and the meaningless fact. Modern philosophy has been an attempt to overcome this antithesis, but, in order to do this, it had in the first place to achieve, as emphatically as possible, consciousness of itself. This has, in fact, been the function of irrationalism in this century. It has, however, tended to disappear as its task has been fulfilled with the further development of twentieth-century philosophy, although it still continues to survive below the level of reflective thought, for example, in various sects and in the cult of parapsychological phenomena. Such 'cults' should not, however, be confused with the scientific study of these phenomena.

The event in itself was, for Lessing, completely meaningless. In his opinion, reason gave meaning to the otherwise meaningless event, with the result that this meaning was arbitrary; hence his statement: 'history was removed from the sphere of the sciences and assigned to the will' (*op. cit.*, 4th edn., p. 3). The rationalism that resulted from Descartes's antithesis was thus worked out in an irrationalism, precisely because this antithesis seemed to Lessing to be untenable. This elaboration took a different form in the case of Klages, who went back to the older division between the spirit, the soul and the body, so as, in the first place, to rectify Descartes's shortcoming with regard to the living and then to contrast this living unity of the soul and body as the saving element, with the spirit as the threatening element. His chief work thus bore the title *Der Geist als Widersacher der Seele* (1929-32).

In Klages's thought, the spirit is radically opposed to life. In his soul, man unconsciously experiences the constantly developing world. By means of his spirit, however, he is able to go out consciously to meet the world. In this, the spirit is not a perfection of the soul, but an analysing and destructive power which is intent on making life impossible. Two meta-physical and completely opposite powers are displayed in the spirit and in life and these powers meet each other in man in a life-and-death struggle. The spirit does not come from life or from the world. It has a different origin and is therefore hostile to life and to the world. Life is constant movement, whereas the spirit is static. The spirit prevents man from experiencing the world by causing a division between the soul and the body. It subjugates nature, sets conscious aims and mechanizes and ultimately kills the spontaneity of life. Klages claimed that this process had reached its climax in our own times and that only if it was ended could the world be saved from disaster.

Irrationalism is rooted in the crisis of understanding. The Cartesian dualism of soul (thought) and body (matter) led to an unequivocal view of understanding, in which understanding as thought (the subject) was directed towards matter as the object. Since Descartes conceived matter as dead matter—even animals had no spontaneity, but were 'machines'—understanding could, in principle, be expressed entirely in concepts. This idea still has force for the neo-positivists, who regard as valid only the logistic way of thinking, in which the Cartesian concept finally becomes a mathematical formula. Klages continued, on the one hand, to identify thought with the concept—in the dualistic tradition of Descartes—although, on the other hand, he rejected Descartes's idea of reality as dead matter and regarded it as living corporeality. For this reason, he was bound to reject thought as a falsification of reality. All the various forms of twentieth-century irrationalism are to some extent in the Cartesian tradition because they remain, in one way or another, within the framework of Descartes's dualism.

It was for this very reason that philosophers like HERMANN KEYSERLING (1880–1946) tried to escape from Western thinking by devoting their attention to the wisdom of the East. But it is not possible to escape from Descartes by avoiding him. The only possible course is to overcome his dualism. Various attempts have in fact been made to do this in contemporary philosophy. The same preoccupation is encountered again and again in neo-Thomism and Marxism, in the different forms of the philosophy of life, in the philosophy of the spirit, in personalism and in existentialism. In their different ways, all the thinkers of these schools have been concerned with the problem of overcoming the antithesis between rationalism and irrationalism, since both are the result of dualism. The distinctive character of twentieth-century philosophy is to a very great extent determined by the restlessness caused by having to put up with both rationalism and irrationalism. Modern philosophers are thus reliving a problem which preoccupied Kant and Hegel in the distinction between intellect (*Verstand*) and reason (*Vernunft*) and, long before them, Thomas Aquinas in the relationship between intellect (*intellectus*) and reason (*ratio*).

5. *Neo-vitalism*

The term 'philosophy of life' has as many meanings as the term 'irrationalism'. It can mean a philosophy which takes life as its central idea or its point of departure: it can also mean a philosophy which sets out to be no more than an expression of life itself. The latter is, in a sense, the case with Bergson, whereas the former is the case with HANS DRIESCH (1867–1941), whose philosophy has often been called neo-vitalism, to distinguish it from earlier forms of vitalism.

For various reasons, Driesch's thought is characteristic of the twentieth century. In the first place, faced with Descartes's dualism, he had to try to overcome this in order to remain in touch with the reality that was its point of departure. In the second place, his thought was an attempt to justify the significance of science and, in particular, that of biology, the central importance of which was becoming more and more evident.

Driesch was originally a biologist and was guided in his first investigations by Haeckel's materialistic monism. In his experiments with sea-urchins, however, he encountered phenomena which could not be mechanically explained and which led him to believe that living phenomena had a structure which was essentially different from that of dead matter and that it was consequently not possible to deduce these living phenomena from lifeless matter. This idea marked the commencement of Driesch's own philosophy and, in a sense, continued to inspire it. So the term 'vitalism' has often been used in connection with Driesch's thought partly because he believed that a special life-force, entelechy, had to be accepted besides the physical and chemical forces at work in the living being.

It is clear straight away how Driesch's point of departure was quite different from that of Klages. For Driesch, philosophy was the 'ordered, systematic knowing of all that is knowable' and had to have its starting-point in something that was not open to doubt. This, for Driesch, was the fact that I *experience* something and, in Driesch's view, experience took place consciously. Driesch therefore defined this primordial experience as: 'I have something consciously.' It was the point of departure for reflection, which in turn discovered that what 'I have consciously' was somehow ordered. Thus the task of philosophy was, for Driesch, the elaboration of the order displayed in what 'I have consciously'. Driesch called this the doctrine of order and he conceived it as logic. Driesch's logic, however, was not simply the formal logic of tradition; it provided also the order of the whole of empirical reality and the whole plan of nature, soul and community as revealed to a man's consciousness. It was only after he had described this order that the philosopher could ask whether this empirical reality was more than his consciousness and, if so, what its nature was.

In the light of the further development of contemporary philosophy, what strikes us today is how Driesch's attempt to break away from idealism was checked halfway. Whereas Klages identified spirit with consciousness and thus opposed it to the unity of the soul and the body, which was not conceived, but experienced, Driesch tried synthetically to preserve the unity of experience and consciousness. He thus saw experience, which played no part in Descartes's thought, or at least in the Cartesianism of the eighteenth and nineteenth centuries, in unity with thought on the one hand and with the body on the other. In this way, he rejected glorification of the unconscious on the one hand and the rationalization of the conscious on the other.

The Cartesian *cogito* occurred in Driesch's thought in the only explicit form in which it could be valid, that is, as *cogito aliquid*, 'I think something', in which thinking was no longer rational and abstract, but living. The neo-Thomists also stressed the *cogito aliquid*, of course, and, both in the neo-Thomist *cogito aliquid* and in Driesch's 'I have something consciously', the twofold division of subject and object remained, these being brought together in the consciousness. The problem that presented itself to the neo-Thomists, who, in their debate with the neo-Kantians, were forced to conclude that whoever began with consciousness was bound to remain enclosed within it, also presented itself to Driesch.

Driesch recognized that reality transcended consciousness, but was this in fact consistent with his point of departure in consciousness, even though, for him, consciousness was consciousness of something? The question that troubled him was this: was consciousness from the very beginning not only consciousness *of* the other thing, but also already consciousness *with* the other thing before it was consciousness with itself? Driesch's struggle with this solipsism shows the extent to which he remained enmeshed within the Cartesian problem of consciousness.

Driesch's thought fluctuated constantly between two poles— that of life on the one hand and metaphysics on the other. These two poles did not repel each other, but kept his thought in constant motion around the central question, what is man? How can man, as conscious experience, as a person, be understood? Reality, Driesch recognized, transcended consciousness, but could only become reality for consciousness if it was itself 'primordially knowing'. This confronted Driesch with the problem of the divine character of reality. Was reality primordially knowing because it was God (pantheism) or was it primordially knowing because it had been created by God (theism)? Driesch maintained that metaphysics could only suggest possibilities, dealing, as it did, with the possibility of reality. But man could not avoid reflecting about the possible.

This, then, metaphysical reflection, was one pole in Driesch's thought. The opposite pole was speculation about life, the activities of which could not, Driesch believed, be explained mechanically. In the case of lifeless things, there was always a partial causality, in which one *part* exerted an influence causally on the other part. Biological research, however, had proved that another form of causality operated in the case of living things—the *whole* living being was always the cause of every activity of whatever part might be involved. Driesch therefore developed the theory of 'totality causality', which operated by virtue of a force which was inherent in living beings only—entelechy. He did not claim that entelechy was a new force in the scientific sense, but that it was the immanent ordering of active physical and chemical forces. Consequently, it did not violate the law of the conservation of energy. It was, however, entelechy which made a totality of the organism and, in Driesch's system, entelechy performed the function which the vegetative or sensitive psyche had for Aristotle and the soul or *anima* had for Thomas and the neo-Thomists.

In his metaphysics, Driesch shared the twentieth-century tendency towards the absolute and the religious view. He did, however, achieve greater clarity than most twentieth-century thinkers in his vitalism, although this aspect of his thought has frequently been misunderstood. What has often not been taken into account is his emphatic statement that entelechy is not a new force in the scientific sense, existing alongside other natural forces. It is simply the immanent order of physical and chemical forces and cannot therefore be thought of quantitatively as something in addition to these forces, but only as something that is, in the totality of the living being, qualitatively *different* from them, although all these forces remain the same in themselves. The problem of analogy—so important in Thomas and Hegel—is clearly of central importance here too. How can the same thing be the same and yet different? This confronts an unequivocal logic with an insurmountable difficulty and it is no coincidence that Driesch regarded his doctrine of order as logic. In his doctrine of reality, of course, he in fact only reached the point of investigating the possibility of reality—this was because he depended, for his point of departure, on Descartes's consciousness.

6. The Philosophy of Evolution

I have deliberately not used the term 'philosophy of life' or 'vitalism' for Bergson's philosophy because it is too ambiguous. The term 'philosophy of evolution' certainly indicates one of the most important tendencies in Bergson's thought, but, in using it, I am running the risk of suggesting that Bergson's philosophy was completely taken up with the idea of evolution. The most accurate name would have been 'philosophy of duration', but the meaning of this term can only be made clear in the course of a discussion of Bergson's thought. It is in any case very important to see Bergson's philosophy from the very outset in the proper perspective, that is, in the tradition of French 'spiritualism'.

HENRI BERGSON (1859–1941) made a resolute stand on the problems of his age in his very first book, *Essai sur les Données Immédiates de la Conscience* (1889), by following the nineteenth-century tradition of refusing to dissociate philosophy from positive science. This recognition of science, which Bergson expressed again and again in his writings, does not, however, imply that he simply accepted the current view of science. A renewal of the interpretation of science can be seen as one of the aims of his philosophy. Bergson's opposition to the mechanistic view of science more or less coincided with the emergence of modern physics. Bergson himself drew attention to this relationship in one of his books, *Durée et Simultanéité* (1922): 'Our admiration for this physicist [that is, Einstein], the conviction that he has given us not only new physics, but also new modes of thought, the idea that natural science and philosophy are different sciences, but have the task of amplifying each other—all this has given us the desire and has even imposed on us the duty to go over to a confrontation' (*op. cit.,* 2nd edn., p. vii). In Bergson's work, this confrontation was not only concerned with natural science—mathematics and biology, physiology and psychology, psychiatry and sociology and history, and the study of comparative religion also played a part in it.

Bergson was, from the very beginning, opposed to determinism and associationism in psychology. In the psychological association of ideas, states of consciousness are called to mind by other states of consciousness—but what are these states of consciousness? They would seem to be abstractions, arbitrary fragments taken out of the stream of consciousness. The consciousness is not static but dynamic and consequently it does not have states, but is in constant movement. The real basis for our thinking of consciousness as a state is our interpretation of time. A great deal has been written about time, but little thought has been given to it. In thought—so Bergson argued—we tend to concentrate on space, analysing this because it can be understood as an idea. We then apply the idea that we have formed of space to time, with the result that time is given dimensions like space and, like space, becomes divisible in units. In this, however, we by-pass reality and create a time that is well suited to (classical) natural science and to our activity in the spatial world, but not suited to an understanding of our consciousness.

Bergson, however, made a distinction between intellect and intuition. Space and physical time were, in Bergson's opinion, products of the schematization of the intellect, which could only grasp the static in its schemes, whereas dynamic time could only be grasped by intuition. Bergson thus kept the term 'time' (*temps*) for physical time and used the term 'duration' (*durée*) for the real time of consciousness.

Consciousness can only be grasped by intuition and understood as duration. Our deeply rooted habit of thinking spatially, however, makes this difficult for us, with the result that our intuition of duration has again and again to be recaptured. By analogy with space, physical time has an extensiveness which duration has not and, like space, physical time is quantitative, whereas duration is qualitative. Consciousness is duration and is consequently qualitative.

If duration is thought of as physical time—with the result that consciousness is also conceived spatially—then it is possible for states of consciousness to be called to mind, through a mechanical process of association, by other states of consciousness. This becomes impossible, however, as soon as consciousness is thought of as duration, from which no quantitative units can be taken without arbitrary abstraction. But this is also important in connection with our idea of freedom. If our psychic life consists of units, by analogy with space, these units are bound to determine each other, as spatial units do. If, however, the idea of quantity is abandoned in connection with the psyche and consciousness can only be conceived qualitatively, determination also ceases to be possible, since determination necessarily takes place within the quantitative and spatial sphere. The freedom of the consciousness is therefore not violated by the determinism of the spatial world.

Spatiality is intimately connected with materiality. Space, quantity and matter form a unity, as Descartes insisted, and, as Descartes once again realized, duration, quality and consciousness also form a unity. It is clear, then, that Bergson fully accepted Descartes's dualism. The antithesis between soul and body was fundamental to Bergson's thought, but his way of looking at this antithesis was different from Descartes's and indeed he saw it in such a way that the antithesis between idealism and realism became weaker. In his book, *Matière et mémoire* (1896), he took his point of departure in 'common sense' (*sens commun*), which recognized both the reality of things and their qualitative character. This point of departure can make the relationship between the soul and the body more intelligible.

As little thought has been given to the relationship between the soul and the body as to the structure of duration. A certain point of view is chosen and the problem itself is overlooked. There are four of these points of view and they are all inadequate. Firstly, it is accepted as satisfactory to speak about the unity of the soul and the body as about an irreducible and inexplicable fact. Secondly, the body is regarded as the instrument of the soul. Thirdly, consciousness is viewed as a phenomenon that is incidental to the function of the brain. Fourthly, there is the point of view that favours parallelism, in that thoughts and the activities of the brain are seen as different expressions of the same fundamental reality.

All these views are inadequate. The activities of the brain express only one aspect of consciousness, namely the aspect of corporeal activity, to which the movement of consciousness can lead. Everything that cannot be expressed corporeally cannot be deduced from the activities of the brain. Physiology therefore can never touch the essential aspect of consciousness. What determines consciousness, then, is *attention to life*, which cannot be derived from physiological data, but which certainly determines the psychological phenomena in which consciousness is manifested. If it is a train of philosophical thought that leads to this conclusion, then all that really emerges from this is the intimate connection between psychology and philosophy, despite their mutual independence. The close relationship between psychology on the one hand and philosophy on the other is surely inevitable, in view of the fact that both sciences are concerned with the human mind, psychology examining its practical activity and philosophy intent on discovering its creative activity.

Just as human consciousness is essentially dynamic and in no sense a state, so too is the whole of reality essentially a dynamic process. In *L'Évolution Créatrice* (1907), therefore, Bergson asserted that life itself was the very basis of all cosmic reality. Life—both that of the cosmos and that of the individual man— is constantly developing. Life is consciousness. It cannot therefore be determined quantitatively like matter, but only qualitatively. A qualitative movement is a dynamism which is continuously bringing forth what is new—it is thus a creative movement. The development of reality can therefore only be conceived as a creative evolution. We share in this creative evolution in our intuition of duration, but we cannot possibly grasp it in spatial and conceptual thought, which is, of necessity, always trying to trace everything that is new back to what has gone before in accordance with the law of deterministic causality. In intuition, however, we are able to experience this continuous renewal as expressed in every creative work and especially in that of the artist.

It is the creative life movement, the *élan vital*, which impels this development onward. It does not, however, move in one direction, but in various directions. It has ceased in lifeless matter, it has discovered different forms of reality in plants and animals and it has found its highest creation in man. Man is himself capable of intervening in this evolution—he is the being who acts, *homo faber*, the being who forms the world. He does this by means of conceptual thought, but thereby runs the risk of interpreting reality entirely in the light of the static concept. This inclination of his intellect is overcome only in his intuition which, in consciousness and reality, discovers duration, which is the real form of being of the *élan vital*.

Even in animals, this *élan vital* displays a tendency towards the formation of communities—bees and ants are the obvious examples of this. But it is in man that the tendency to form communities is most fully developed. He forms closed communities, but there is also the open human community. The closed community is restricted to a definite group and its members are 'joined by mutual bonds, always ready to attack or to defend and tied to an attitude of combat'. The open community, on the other hand, 'embraces in principle the whole of mankind'. This is how Bergson himself defined the contrast between the closed and the open community in his last book, *Les Deux Sources de la Morale et de la Religion* (1932, pp. 287–8). The closed community has a closed morality, a morality of social obligations which imposes restraint on the individual and keeps him within the restricted confines of the community. The open community, on the other hand, has an open morality, a morality of love by means of which the human person can develop fully.

The problem of morality leads to the question of religion. There is no morality of the community without at the same time a religion which ensures the unity of the community. Without religion, morality would not survive and, without morality, the community itself would not endure. That is why closed religion can be described as 'a defensive reaction of nature against the activity of the intellect insofar as this oppresses the individual and dissolves the community' (*op. cit.*, p. 219). When he wrote this, Bergson once again had the conceptual and technical intellect in mind. In contrast to this static, closed religion, however, there is also dynamic, open religion and, whereas static religion keeps life at the level that it has already attained, dynamic religion takes life on towards its full development in love. Love of men is intimately related to love of God, towards which mankind is moving. This love reaches its highest form in Christian mysticism and the mystic is the one who 'loves the whole of mankind with divine love through God and by virtue of God' (*op. cit.*, p. 249).

The great problems of the turn of the century were expressed for the first time and in a most impressive way in the philosophy of Henri Bergson. He included positive science within the framework of philosophical thought, but at the same time insisted on the freedom of both. He took the idea of evolution to its ultimate conclusion, but also thought out deeply and consistently the relationship between man and God. While stressing the irreducible and distinctive character of man as an individual person, he did not fail to emphasize the individual's intimate bond with society. Whereas he fully recognized the validity of rational thought, he also expressed the mysterious character of reality. He accorded a central position to biology in reality, but at the same time gave priority to the spirit. Finally, although he saw action and understanding as inter-related, he also strongly affirmed and developed the idea of intuitive insight.

There was certainly an element of fashionable snobbery in the great admiration for Bergson that was felt during the years between the publication of his two last great books. Since then, however, the great depth and breadth of his answer to the philosophical problems of our age has become more and more apparent. No twentieth-century philosophical movement has remained outside his influence. To some extent, all contemporary thinking about time, life, man, the community, morality and religion has been determined by him. It has also become increasingly clear how wrong it is to speak about irrationalism in connection with Bergson's thought. His insistence on intuition as the purest expression of the *élan vital* does not in any sense mean that intuition is an irrational force, since life is consciousness. The same tension is present in the antithesis between Bergson's intelligence and intuition as there was in Thomism between intellect (*intellectus*) and reason (*ratio*) and, in Kant and Hegel, between intellect (*Verstand*) and reason (*Vernunft*). Husson was not wrong to entitle the book that he wrote about Bergson (published in 1947) *L'Intellectualisme de Bergson*. The idea that Bergson's intention was to advocate irrationalism did not originate, however, in France, where his position within the spiritualistic tradition was easily recognized, but in the Germanic countries, where his thought was misinterpreted because of a lack of knowledge of the French philosophical tradition.

A return to the works of Bergson himself has not been rendered superfluous by his influence on later spiritualism and existentialism, in both of which movements central themes of his philosophy have been further elaborated. His inspiration is still very important, for a great philosopher has this in common with a great artist—quite apart from the influence that he may have on others, his work always retains its originality, so that it remains new whenever it is approached anew. In the case of Bergson, there are no signs of any imminent disappearance of this newness. On the contrary, it looks as though there is a real need to study Bergson's themes again with renewed interest.

Although no school ever formed itself round Bergson, his thought has been a source of inspiration to many thinkers and, in particular, to two philosophers who applied their minds especially to the problem of evolution. These are EDOUARD LE ROY (1870–1954) and PIERRE TEILHARD DE CHARDIN (1881–1955).

Le Roy and Teilhard were bound together by such close bonds of friendship that it is possible to speak, in their case, of a common philosophy. Both were concerned with the problem of evolution, although each looked at it from his own point of view. Le Roy considered it from the point of view of Bergson's philosophy, with which he was thoroughly familiar. Teilhard saw it from the scientific point of view of palaeontology. Le Roy's two books on this theme, *L'Exigence Idéaliste et le Fait de l'Evolution* (1927) and *Les Origines Humaines et l'Evolution de l'Intelligence* (1928), are still extremely important in connection with any philosophy of evolution. Where Teilhard's philosophical ideas do not reflect his own philosophical and theological education, they echo Le Roy's philosophical ideas. In the works of Teilhard that have been published so far, his idea of evolution is expressed in the most synthetic way in *Le Phénomène Humain* (1955) and his religious thought in *Le Milieu Divin* (1957).

A scientific approach to the world in which we live requires a new method besides (or between) that of positive science on the one hand and philosophy on the other. In this approach, it is a question of seeing the great outlines of evolving reality. Teilhard therefore spoke of phenomenology or hyper-physics. Evolution embraces the whole of reality. There is continuity between cosmic, vital and human (cultural) evolution. This continuity at the same time implies discontinuity—which comes into being in the course of evolution. The living arises from the lifeless, but it is at the same time qualitatively different from the lifeless. Man arises from the pre-human, but he is at the same time more than the pre-human.

Evolution is therefore progress. In the sphere of life, the guiding line is cephalization, the development of the brain. There is a parallel between the higher development of the cerebral and nervous system and the higher development of consciousness. In this context, Teilhard used the term *la loi de complexité-conscience*, the law of the associated complexity of bodily structure and consciousness. All further progress can therefore be typified as the growth of freedom and, because evolution has led to man, previous evolution can be regarded as growth towards freedom.

In view of the movement of evolution, there is no reason for us to expect any reversal of this process, leading to the decline of mankind. It is, however, true to say that evolution gains a new dimension with freedom, so that it becomes no longer unconscious, but conscious. Man thus takes his evolution into his own hands and so can even end it. In this way the doctrine of evolution acquires the character of an appeal to human freedom. Christians and non-Christians can find each other in consciously working for the progress of the world. They can be sustained in this task by the awareness that man's longing for unity, truth, authenticity and justice has never been so great at any other period of history as it is now.

Unity is ultimately reached, not on the basis of an abstract ideal, but on the basis of a fully human solidarity, love. Christ therefore appears as the 'point omega', as the one who attracts all humanity towards himself and makes it one. Faith in Christ does not draw man away from his terrestrial task, but rather confirms him in this task. The material, biological reality is deified in Christ and is thereby not done away with, but rather assigned to man as his special sphere.

7. The Philosophy of Action

Round about the turn of the century, Western man felt the need to think about his action—what did he want with his science, his politics, his everyday activities? This became an increasingly urgent problem for more and more people when the apparent equilibrium of the world was shaken by the First World War and the powers of destruction were revealed with increasing clarity. Yet, even at the end of the nineteenth century, some thinkers had already seen the questions that were to be everyone's problem fifty years later. The whole of the philosophical activity of MAURICE BLONDEL (1861–1949) was an investigation into the meaning of human action. The essence of his thought is all to be found in L'Action (1893). At an advanced age, he elaborated his thought in the trilogy, La Pensée (1934), L'Être et les Êtres (1935) and L'Action (1936–7), but the fundamental ideas were the same as those expressed in the earlier work.

William James quoted Blondel in the preface to his Pragmatism of 1907 because of the affinity between Blondel's thought and his own. Both philosophers certainly analysed action and emphasized its fundamental importance. But there are great differences between them. James analysed action in its utility. Utility for James was determined not only by material usefulness, but also by everything that was of service to man, from material use to art, philosophy and religion. Blondel, on the other hand, analysed action as a structure of man's being. For Blondel, man *was* action and therefore provided an ontology. James situated man—in view of the emphasis that he gave to usefulness to man—centrally in reality, following in this sense certain tendencies of idealism. Blondel, however, regarded man as ex-centric and saw his action as, consciously or unconsciously, directed towards God. The similarities and differences between James and Blondel become strikingly apparent when James's *Varieties of Religious Experience* (his Gifford lectures of 1901–2) is compared with Blondel's *La Philosophie et l'Esprit Chrétien* (1944–6). Or is this an unfair comparison, since James's is an early work and Blondel's is a very late work and Blondel had, moreover, been able to assimilate Bergson's *Les Deux Sources de la Morale et de la Religion*?

Blondel's investigation into human action was, from the very outset, an investigation into the *meaning* of this action. There is an inner finality in action—everyone performs a definite action with a definite aim. Thus, one action is performed for the sake of another. This, however, does not explain action in itself; it only accounts for the definite character of actions. Action itself, as the total activity of man, in which thought and will are also implied, demands a meaning. This means that the problem of the meaningfulness of a definite action ultimately confronts us with the problem of action itself or, expressed in another way, with the problem of the meaning of life itself. This problem cannot be avoided since thought is implicit in all action. Man is only fully man when he

H

makes such implicit thought explicit in a conscious action. Not all action can, of course, take place completely consciously, but the ideal certainly holds good that the conscious character of action should be approached as closely as possible and, what is more, this consciousness does not necessarily destroy the spontaneity of action. This conscious nature of action means that man accepts full responsibility for his action and this responsibility in turn confronts him with the problem of the meaning of everything that he does, in other words, it faces him with the question as to why he is living.

It is, then, ultimately a question of whether our life is meaningful or meaningless. *Within* our life, a definite action may be either meaningful or meaningless, but the total decision about the meaningfulness of our life as such cannot be situated within our life—it must transcend our life. Our life is either orientated towards a personal God, whom we strive to approach, or it is not. It is only in the first case that it is possible for us to make life really meaningful. In the second case, everything is ultimately meaningless. If, however, our life is directed towards a personal God, this relationship cannot be destroyed by death. There must therefore be a mode of continued existence for man which does not make his striving to come nearer to God and the perfection that is attained in this striving completely meaningless. The whole of religion and morality and even all intellectual action therefore calls for a continued existence, if it is not to be meaningless.

This question is never presented in the abstract. It always emerges from the concrete situation of a particular man living within a spatially and temporally determined world. Religion also reveals itself within this world and it is religion which provides the answer to man's question about the meaning of life. Philosophical thought therefore confronts us with the religious question and shows us that human responsibility compels us to investigate the message which religion, and

Christianity in particular, brings to us. This is clearly a question of rejection or acceptance, but this decision no longer lies within the sphere of philosophy.

Blondel himself gave several indications in his later years that his thought anticipated existentialism. There are indeed certain basic features common to both Blondel's philosophy and existentialism. Both are concerned with the *being* of man and reality. Both share the view that man's being betrays a meaning which does not easily come to explicit consciousness, but has, as it were, to be brought to consciousness. Depth psychology exerted a considerable influence here in the case of existentialism, but not, of course, on Blondel's *L'Action* of 1893, since Freud's first work had not then appeared. It is, however, difficult to say with certainty whether Blondel had any direct influence on the existentialist philosophers. It is a plausible supposition in the case of Marcel. Heidegger certainly read *L'Action* when he was a young man. Jaspers presumably never read Blondel's work and the climate of Sartre's thought is undoubtedly too far removed from Blondel's work for us to consider the possibility of any influence.

On the other hand, Blondel had a very great influence on the French and Italian philosophy of spirit and on later neo-Thomism. Problems of religious philosophy occupied a central position in Blondel's thought. Like Bergson, he gave a great deal of attention to mysticism. Again and again he raised the question of the relationship between faith and thought, between theology and philosophy. Under his influence, the neo-Thomists abandoned their original division between faith and thought. They did not, however, take up the theme of his last book, that of a philosophical thinking out of Christian dogmatism, in which this dogmatism continues to be an expression of faith and the philosophical consideration of it remains philosophically aloof, in accordance with Husserl's reduction, and thus does not itself become theology.

There was a great deal of resistance at the Sorbonne in 1893 to Blondel's argument, on the basis of the conviction that action could not be the subject of philosophical reflection. This made it necessary for Blondel to clarify the relationships between thought and action. Investigation into consciousness, into what consciousness is aware of and into what it is not aware of, occupied an important place in this. For a proper understanding of this problem within the tradition of French philosophy and indeed within the German philosophical tradition of the *Bewusztsein* as well, it should not be forgotten that the French *conscience* signifies in indivisible unity both consciousness and conscience. This means that the French *mouvement de la conscience* is quite different from the German *Bewegung des Bewusztseins*—it is concerned with the whole of man's being and not simply with a knowing which may possibly remain pure theory.

Like Bergson, Blondel expressed the twentieth-century desire to see the relative, precisely because it is relative, related to the absolute. 'All attempts to perfect human action fail and yet this action of necessity strives to satisfy itself and to perfect itself. It cannot do otherwise and yet it always fails.'[1] Blondel's failing (*échouer*) is similar to Jaspers's failing (*Scheitern*), but Blondel was more concrete in his elaboration of the meaning of failure. The sub-title that Blondel gave to his early work was *Essai d'une Critique de la Vie et d'une Science de la Pratique*. Leaving aside any consideration of the extent to which this sub-title reveals that Blondel wanted to provide an answer to Kant's problem, it should be noted that Blondel clarified it later in the book as follows: 'Criticism of life, when it sets out to solve the human problem, cannot avoid attempting to solve the universal problem at the same time. It determines the common meeting-point of science, morality and metaphysics.

[1] *L'Action*, 321.

It establishes the relationships between knowledge and reality. It defines the meaning of being. It discovers this vital point at the intersection of knowing and willing, in action.'[2]

This definition shows quite clearly that Blondel was, like Bergson, in no sense an irrationalist. In 1948, Henry Duméry wrote his *Essai sur l'Intellectualisme Blondélien* with which Blondel himself was, on his own explicit admission, in agreement. Whereas Bergson tried to make Descartes's dualism acceptable Blondel attempted to overcome it. He acknowledged the distinction between perception and thought and between striving and willing, but insisted that the one is never present, in concrete human action, without the other. He maintained that the unity of spirit and matter in man is reflected in man's concrete action, which is always an expression of his being bound to this world and of the *élan* with which he, consciously or unconsciously, orientates himself towards God. Blondel, like Bergson, did not establish a school of philosophy, but the problems with which he was concerned were elaborated by other thinkers, including his pupils, JACQUES PALIARD (1887–1953) and AUGUSTE VALENSIN (1879–1953).

8. *The Philosophy of Spirit*

The term 'philosophy of spirit' (or 'spiritualism') can be used in a narrow and in a wide sense. In its narrow sense, it applies to the whole tradition that has dominated French philosophy since the time of Montaigne, Descartes and Pascal, a tradition from which no later French thinker has held himself completely aloof. It is, however, meaningful to apply the name 'spiritualist' only to those philosophers for whom spirit is the determining reality. It is, of course, possible that this may lead to idealism, but this has, in fact, seldom happened and the

[2]*Op. cit.,* 480.

philosophy of spirit has, for the most part, tended towards realism, recognizing equally the reality of matter and that of spirit, but insisting on the priority of spirit as, so to speak, the ultimate inward goal of matter.

In its wider sense, the name 'philosopher of spirit' or 'spiritualist' could be applied to all those thinkers who, in their work, acknowledge this priority, but, in that case, the term would be no more than a collective name for nearly all European philosophers. It is therefore meaningful to consider this term only against the background of a definite philosophical tradition. If the French spiritualist tradition has to a great extent been determined by Augustine via Descartes and Pascal, then it is possible to say that all the philosophical movements that have been powerfully influenced by Augustine are philosophies of spirit. It is, however, necessary to limit ourselves here to spiritualism in the narrow sense of the word, that is, to the French movement known as the 'philosophy of spirit' as developed by LOUIS LAVELLE (1883–1951) and RENÉ LE SENNE (1882–1954). Other forms of French spiritualism have already been dealt with in the sections on the criticism of science and on Bergson and Blondel, and further forms will be discussed later in this book in the sections on personalism and existentialism.

The term *philosophie de l'esprit* was originally no more than the name given to a series of books edited by Lavelle and Le Senne. So distinctive, however, was the thought that emerged from this series of philosophical works that the term soon came to be used among philosophers as the accepted name for the philosophy of Lavelle, Le Senne and those whose ideas were closely related to theirs.

The philosophy of spirit was influenced by Brunschvicg and especially by the fact that its opposition to his idealistic positivism enabled it to come to an understanding of itself. It was also directly inspired by the thought of Bergson and

Blondel and by the idealism of OCTAVE HAMELIN (1856–1907). Both Lavelle and Le Senne were constantly involved in an argument with Hamelin's thought. Le Senne's aim was to remain faithful to idealism while at the same time assimilating existential experience. For this reason, he called his own thought 'ideo-existentialism'. Lavelle, on the other hand, aimed to overcome the antithesis between idealism and realism. The tension between idealism and realism was already present in the thought of Hamelin himself, whose aim was to remain fully and integrally an idealist, but at the same time to come, via idealism, to the recognition of a personal God.

Hamelin attempted to provide, in his *Essai sur les Éléments Principaux de la Représentation* (1907), a philosophical system in which all known facts and all facts that still remained to be known would have their place. Such a system could only be one of relations, since, for Hamelin, the only reality was that of the relation. The relation itself was furthermore, in Hamelin's view, simply an act of thought, with the result that thought was the only reality. Hamelin's system of relations, in accordance with a dialectical thinking in which an antithesis was constantly overcome at a higher level, led from the abstract to the concrete, so that the concrete human person stood at the summit of this dialectical train of thought. Man, however, was, for Hamelin, a limited being and thought consequently needed to recognize a more perfect reality above human reality. This had also to be a person and, in this way, Hamelin came to a theistic concept of God.

Hamelin's thought displays an apparently close affinity with that of Hegel, but, in fact, he was unacquainted with Hegel's philosophy. In his dialectical thought, he was more influenced by Fichte, whereas the central position which he gave to relation is strongly reminiscent of Bradley, although he and Bradley were not familiar with each other's work.

In a very well thought out manner, Hamelin confronted

twentieth-century French philosophy with the problem of idealism, but it was not only this that inspired Lavelle and Le Senne. Together with Hamelin, they wished to vindicate philosophically the freedom of the human person and his involvement with a personal God. Lavelle attempted to do this in his *Dialectique de l'Eternel Présent,* a work conceived on a grand scale (1928–51). Le Senne's most important work was *Obstacle et Valeur* (1934).

Le Senne was firmly convinced that human existence could only be realized in the overcoming of resistance. For him human existence was to be found in the constant realization of values which had to be gained in a struggle against resistance. He claimed that this constant tension between value and resistance was displayed by consciousness and that philosophy was the description of consciousness—*la description de conscience.* He deliberately omitted the article because to call philosophy the description of *the* consciousness would be to separate description and consciousness.

The philosophical description is itself an act of consciousness. There is no distance between the description and what is described because the two are identical. Both the description and what is described are the same act of consciousness. Philosophy is concerned with the identity of consciousness with itself. This identity is, however, never absolute—there is always tension between the activity of the subject, the ego, and the given nature of the object. To allow everything to become merged into the ego and thus to adhere to an absolute idealism is just as dangerous as to forget the part played by the ego and thus to regard reality as the sum of the objects. An object is, after all, only present for a subject.

Le Senne criticized Hamelin for forgetting this tension and therefore for neglecting to take into account the limits of the ego which can only find itself in the resistance of reality. In his description of consciousness, Le Senne strove to experience the limits of the ego and thus the limits of human thought. Together with James, he maintained that human knowledge was contained within the framework of experience, but he took experience in its widest sense, to include mystical experience. He insisted that an aspect of totality, making everything related to everything else, was always present in experience, with the result that empiricism, which regarded experiences as separate data, was, for him, philosophically untenable.

Le Senne's idealism is quite different from the traditional German idealism. His idealism, expressing man's experience of reality as *conscience*, that is, as consciousness which, as conscience, determines action, is directly orientated towards the personal vindication of existence. Man's life is not determined either by an absolute spirit which is at work within him or by an equally absolute matter which impels him blindly forward. Man chooses his path freely and consciously and every obstacle is the cause of deeper realization or at least offers the possibility of this. Human reality is never given—it forms itself in the tension between the world from which it moves and God, towards whom it is moving.

Lavelle has sometimes been called the last of the classical philosophers. He was entirely concerned with the problem of being and his thought clearly reveals the inspiration of Plotinus. Philosophy is only meaningful if it implies contact with the Absolute. The Absolute is Being. We are constantly encountering Being for, even though we might attempt to reduce the whole of reality to the level of a phenomenon, this phenomenon would still *be*. Being is the creative activity from which everything flows—it is *acte pur*. Insofar as we ourselves are actual, we share in it and are secure in it. Every being shares in this Being and this sharing is not an identification, but, precisely as participation, remains separated from Being by a distance. This participation becomes known to each of us in a fundamental experience, that of the mutual presence of myself to Being and of Being to myself. I do not become merged with Being in this presence, because the distance remains in the form of the world, to which man is tied in this life.

Morality is determined by participation—it is a constant striving to bridge the gap, the distance separating the participation of every being in Being from Being itself. Although this striving cannot gain its object, it does result in man's coming nearer and nearer to Being. This approaching is love, the deepest driving force in man. It is through love that man discovers that Being is God. Love, however, realizes itself not only in mysticism—there is also love of one's fellowmen. Man is essentially not an individual and it is in the other man that he first finds himself. But, just as I am separated from Being by a distance, so too am I separated from the other man by a distance. It is, however, precisely this distance, the world, that at the same time binds us together. There is a dialectic which cannot be cancelled out in man's relationship with God, with the other man and with the world. It is in the world that man finds God as the pure act which sustains the world, but, at the same time, the world comes between God and man. This irreducible dialectic thus results in a gap between man and God which can only be bridged in man's love for his fellowmen in the world, for it is by means of this love that the world reveals its being from God.

It would at first sight seem as though Lavelle's thought was quite remote from the central problem of the twentieth century. In fact, however, this philosopher was deeply concerned with a highly contemporary problem—how does man find God, Being, the Absolute? Does not God stand in the way of man's love for other men or is the truth precisely the opposite—that man's love of his fellow men has its foundation and meaning only in his love of God? The very same problem concerned Le Senne, but, because he dealt with it in a much more concrete way, his thought appeals far more readily to modern man. There may be a great deal in Lavelle's philosophy which the neo-positivist would characterize as poetry, but the problem that Lavelle posed is precisely the one that has always preoccupied philosophers.

The philosophy of spirit has played a very important part in contemporary French philosophy and has had an equally powerful influence on Italian thought. In Italy, the influence of the French philosophy of spirit has coincided with that of Gentile and Blondel, giving rise to Italian spiritualism, the best known representative of which is MICHELE SCIACCA (b. 1908).

9. *Personalism*

The term personalism is used to denote the thought of a group of French philosophers, among whom EMMANUEL MOUNIER (1905–50) and DENIS DE ROUGEMONT (b. 1906) occupy a central position. The same term, personalism, could also be applied to the thought of a number of German philosophers, because they too were fundamentally concerned with the significance of the human person. RUDOLF EUCKEN (1846–1926) and, with even greater justice, WILLIAM STERN (1871–1938), OTHMAR SPANN (1878–1950), PETER WUST (1884–1940), ROMANO GUARDINI (b. 1885) and THEODOR HAECKER (1879–1945) would have to be included among the German personalists. The essential themes of all these French and German philosophers were the relationship between man and the world, the meaning of personal freedom, and the significance of the individual person's link with the human community. Here, however, I shall have to limit myself to French personalism, which derives its contemporary importance and appeal from the way in which it approaches the dialogue between philosophy and concrete reality.

In the thought of both Mounier and De Rougemont, we find a fundamental conviction, as deep as that of Marx, that human society must, of necessity, be renewed. In this new society, the human person will not, however, be allowed to become subjugated to society, as is, in fact, the case with dialectical materialism and as is indeed also the case, although the way in which this takes place is different, in contemporary bourgeois society. On the contrary, society will have to be so organized that the individual person can, in freedom, be fully himself. This does not imply that the person is isolated from the community, but that he can only live fully in and for the community if he is not completely absorbed in it. It is only if both the community and the individual person recognize a personal God that the value and dignity of the human person can be guaranteed. Otherwise, there is always the threat that he will become the victim of power, whether the power of the state, of capital or of a definite class.

This problem was and still is discussed in a very concrete manner in the journal *Esprit* which was founded by Mounier and has been continued, since his death, by Albert Béguin and Jean Lacroix. Personalism has accepted Marx's conviction that philosophy must change the world, but, unlike Marxism, it does not offer a fully thought out programme of action. It maintains that man must base his programme of action on the concrete and constantly developing situation. This does not, however, mean that there are no guiding principles indicating the direction in which this action should lie. Both the dignity of the individual person and the well-being of the human community are at stake in such action and these two are not independent of each other, but are rather the condition of each other.

The dignity of the person is above all to be found in his freedom. The tragic aspect of Marxism is that it does not know what to do with individual freedom and consequently always tries, in practice, to destroy it. It would, however, be a serious error of judgement to think that Western society, on the other hand, fully guarantees the freedom of the individual. The structure of Western society is such that what Marx called alienation has become a reality in the full sense of the word. Western man devotes his activity to the attainment of ends which he himself does not wish to achieve, but which he is bound to serve in order to make sure of his material existence.

Marxism is right in establishing an intimate connection not only between philosophy, politics and economics, but also between philosophy and the various sciences. This second connection is a perfectly legitimate one, since both philosophy and society are only able to develop by means of the sciences. But the inherent danger present in Marxism is that it has an *a priori* conception both of science and of society and as little respect for the freedom of science as it has for the freedom of human society. In contrast to Marxism, personalism strives to remain open to the further development of science.

Personalism also differs from Marxism in its attitude towards religion. Marxism rejects religion as the ideology of the capitalist class. Personalism, on the other hand, regards religion as the motive force which makes man morally conscious. Since this moral consciousness is, of its very nature, directed towards society—authentic morality always furthers the togetherness of man—any check placed on religion inevitably checks the free growth of moral responsibility and thus the development of human activity directed towards the constant and progressive improvement and renewal of the human community.

The well-being of the community cannot be specified *a priori* in the concrete. It is brought about in the social work of the members of the community themselves. All that can be positively said is that the well-being of the community includes both its spiritual and its material life. The material existence of the human community calls in the first place for a raising of the standard of living of part of the population of Europe and of by far the greater part of the population of the world. It therefore calls for a just distribution of the world's riches and for peace, since war threatens the material well-being of the human community as well as its spiritual well-being. The personalists therefore insist on the removal of the last traces of colonialism and imperialism and on the realization of world peace on the basis of national independence.

The spiritual life of the human community calls not only for the spiritual freedom of the members of each community, but also for openness on the part of each community to the other communities. Religion and philosophy, art and science—these can only be born of freedom. They can all contribute to the process of making mankind one, but only if they are allowed to develop in freedom. The well-being of the community is, after all, ultimately the well-being of the whole world. It is impossible to speak of the well-being of the world while poverty or hunger is still present in the world or so long as freedom is still absent from any part of it.

There is always a dialectical tension between man's spiritual life and the material conditions under which he lives. An all-absorbing concern for his material existence will inevitably kill his spirit, but this concern can have two different causes. In the first place, the very structure of society may force man to care exclusively for his material existence and, in this case, there is a clear duty to change this society. But, in the second place, man may also choose to concern himself exclusively with his material existence because he is not primarily seeking what is necessary to life, but is pursuing a superabundance of wealth or personal power. A renewal of society cannot change this inner direction of man's will, but it can be alert to it and guard against the possibility of wealth and power falling into the hands of individuals. Both political and socio-economic democracy are therefore necessary.

If, however, man has sufficient to ensure his own and his fellows' material existence, this sufficiency then acts as a first condition for the development of his spiritual life, provided that he is strong enough to resist the urge to go on devoting himself exclusively to the improvement of his material existence. The second condition, then, for spiritual wealth is a voluntary turning away from material superabundance. This can only be achieved in the mean between material need and material abundance, if this mean is voluntarily chosen in conscious renunciation.

In his *Penser avec les Mains* (1936), Denis de Rougemont defined personalism as follows: 'Civilization's mission is to lead a revolution which will otherwise be directed against it. To bring about this revolution, it is necessary to find out and recognize a criterion which is common to both thought and action, to both the élite and the people who will have to help this élite. It is above all a question of bringing this criterion to life by acts and of reforming the world according to the image of this criterion' (p. 196).

As Mounier said in his *Manifeste au Service du Personalisme* (1936), 'We call every doctrine and every civilization personalistic if it recognizes the primacy of the human person above the material necessities and the collective institutions which sustain the development of the individual' (p. 7). There is, however, no separation of the individual person and the community implied in personalistic philosophy: as Mounier emphatically stated later in the same work, 'The modern world's tendency to become impersonal and the decline of the idea of the community point, in our view, to the same process of disintegration' (p. 81). In this, he was alluding to the contrast between the personalistic and the Marxist ideas of history. Both reject bourgeois and fascist society and both aim at the creation of a new society. The Marxist, however, remains tied to the determinism of the nineteenth century, believing that the new society will come whatever happens. The personalist, on the other hand, is convinced that a new society will only come when man chooses to bring it about. For the personalist, history is not a fact which happens to mankind, but something that mankind must make.

10. *Phenomenology*

Contemporary philosophy has been very deeply influenced by the phenomenology of EDMUND HUSSERL (1859–1938). Like the neo-Kantians, Husserl took his point of departure in the theory of science. He was originally a mathematician and became aware of the need for an ever broadening basis for the theoretical problems with which he, as a mathematician, was confronted. This led him to a decisive insight—that the first step towards any attempt to understand these problems had to be appropriate access to the phenomena themselves. Phenomenology thus evolved as the method of approaching phenomena in their pure state. This has always remained the guiding principle in the whole development of Husserl's phenomenology.

What is a phenomenon? For Husserl, it was anything, imagined or objectively existing, ideal or real, that presented itself in any way to man's consciousness. Husserl's aim was to work out a method which would not falsify these phenomena, but would allow them to be described as they appeared. He thus attempted to approach phenomena without any prejudices, theories or presuppositions and to see them as they were in themselves—to go to the things themselves (*zu den Sachen selbst*).

This return to things in themselves, however, continued to be a return to things as they appeared to consciousness—a phenomenon was, for Husserl, a thing appearing in the consciousness. In his earliest period, however, this did not mean that, as idealism maintained, these things were nothing more than the forms in which consciousness appeared. This would have implied the introduction of a theory and Husserl insisted at this stage that phenomenology had to be pre-theoretical. Neither did it mean that Husserl was a realist, since phenomenology preceded the distinction between realism and idealism.

If there was to be a return to the phenomena themselves, however, a guiding principle of method was required. Husserl realized that it was impossible to describe phenomena in their individual details and, even if this were possible, it would be quite meaningless. He therefore concluded that it was necessary to try to grasp the essence of the phenomena—the phenomenological method had to leave what was inessential aside and to allow the essence of the phenomena to speak for itself. This was not an abstraction, but an intuition of the essence itself (*Wesenserschauung*). Husserl always regarded the problem of method as fundamental, and the central theme of all his philosophical writings—of his early work, *Logische Untersuchungen* (1900–1), for example, in which he put forward for the first time the programme of his phenomenology, and of his later work—was that of the phenomenological method. He applied this method in the concrete to various spheres of being far more frequently, however, in the work that was published after his death.

One of Husserl's leading ideas was that of intentionality. Human consciousness can never be directly grasped in itself because it is essentially intentional, that is, directed towards that which is not in itself consciousness. Perceptions and concepts, ideas and fantasies, desires and aspirations—all these are always intentional, in other words, directed towards something. It is only by analysing this intentionality that consciousness itself can be discovered. Husserl's disciples were led above all by this idea of intentionality to realism, although

I

Husserl himself gradually tended towards idealism. The precise nature of this idealism is, however, still open to dispute.

This tendency towards idealism emerged clearly for the first time in Husserl's *Ideen zu einer reinen Phänomenologie und phänomenologischen Philosophie* (1913). The phenomenologist has very firmly to place the reality of the outside world 'between brackets' or 'exclude' it. He is concerned with the phenomenon and the phenomenon reveals itself only in consciousness. A suitable method is required for this exclusion of the outside world because the spontaneous notion of the outside world is always imperceptibly penetrating and falsifying the analysis. This phenomenological method is put into practice in the process of 'reduction' or *epoche*. The first reduction is the eidetic reduction, which enables the essence (*eidos*) in the phenomenon to be seen. The second is the transcendental reduction, which places every relation between the phenomenon and the outside world between brackets. It is possible, by means of these two reductions, to reach transcendental consciousness, of which empirical consciousness is always the special form of expression.

As a method, phenomenology is a preparation for all philosophical investigation and research into the positive sciences. In examining the essence of each science, it discovers the basic structure of being of that science and thus becomes a regional ontology. The unity of these regional ontologies is given in formal ontology.

In his *Formale und transzendentale Logik* (1929), Husserl once more considered the problem that had preoccupied him in his earlier book, *Logische Untersuchungen,* and thus again took up the cudgels against psychologism, maintaining that it was impossible for logic to be absorbed completely by psychology since, whereas psychology could describe the factual course of acts of thought, only logic could judge their validity. At the same time, he also discussed a problem which was to play an increasingly important part in his later works, including the *Méditations Cartésiennes* (1931). If, in order to discover transcendental consciousness in my own consciousness, I take my own consciousness as my point of departure, how do I encounter others in this consciousness? Do I not, in this case, fall into solipsism, with the result that nothing *is* other than my own consciousness? How, then, can I have any knowledge of an inter-subjective world?

Consideration of this question brought Husserl face to face, during the last period of his life, with the problem of the concrete world in which man lived (the *Lebenswelt*). He found himself compelled to reconsider the concrete outside world that had been set aside by his earlier pre-occupation with eidetic reduction and to reconsider, at the same time, the problem of history. Husserl placed great emphasis, at this stage of his development, on the fact that the concrete world in which man lived was the world which had been fashioned by history and that it was only possible to understand this world fully in the light of its historical growth: full understanding seemed to him to be all the more necessary because this world was in a state of crisis, the crisis of the sciences being only one of the forms in which a greater crisis expressed itself. He developed this theme in his *Die Krisis der europäischen Wissenschaften* (1936).

There are certain constant factors in Husserl's work and there are also themes which reveal a gradual shift of emphasis. One of the constant elements in his thought was the conviction that the whole philosophical problem had to be built up again from the foundations. In this, Husserl came to feel himself more and more closely related to Descartes, who was also convinced of this in the seventeenth century. He also shared with Descartes the first belief that philosophy had to be built up as a strict science. In his opinion, unanimity was both possible and necessary in philosophy, on condition that philosophy was conducted along strictly scientific lines. This did not, for him, mean that philosophy and the positive sciences were not essentially different, but it did mean that it was possible to use a formal method, namely phenomenology, which would provide the basic guiding principles for the different methods of philosophy and the positive sciences. Every scientific method was, for Husserl, a specialization of the universally valid phenomenological method.

Husserl's idea of intentionality, however, did not remain constant. The stress that he laid on the intentional nature of human consciousness had a liberating effect, but this intentionality became more and more dubious as he placed increasing emphasis on the tendency to allow phenomenology to describe the content of consciousness as conscious. There were, in fact, only two possible ways out of this dilemma—either to regard consciousness as the only reality to be investigated (the solution offered by idealism) or, at the very outset, to place intentionality in the world (the way followed by Heidegger).

Husserl's idea of intuition of the essence of phenomena also displayed a curve. How is it possible to deduce the essence of a phenomenon from its empirical fullness and its changeable nature? This empirical reality at first tended to play a less important part in Husserl's thought than his idea of intuition of the essence itself, but later he became more and more aware of the fact that his principle of intentionality could not be reconciled with this. There was always the danger of consciousness becoming an abstract consciousness in no way related to concrete consciousness. It was this that led Husserl to consider, in his later works, the problem of the concrete world in which man lives, the *Lebenswelt*.

Husserl's attitude towards idealism was also uncertain. He opened the way to realism for his disciples, but tended himself towards idealism, thereby to a very great extent losing his grip on his disciples. The most independent among these were those who studied under him during the first ten years or so of this century. Husserl's later concern with the *Lebenswelt* was a confrontation with realism. Did it imply a change of direction towards realism? Or was his idealism never in fact idealism in the classical sense of the word, but simply a methodical idealism, just as Descartes's doubt was a methodical doubt? But can this methodical idealism be reconciled with the idea of intentionality? Does this idea call, not for a placing of the outside world between brackets, but a placing of the consciousness between brackets? Do the questions of eidetic reduction, idealism and transcendental consciousness not bear a very close relationship to each other and does the impossibility of one of these points of view not imply the untenability of the others?

These are some of the questions posed by Husserl's phenomenology. It is impossible to tell *a priori* the extent to which these questions are answered in Husserl's posthumous work the publication of which has already been commenced, although it is by no means completed. What is becoming increasingly clear, however, is that Husserl was a transitional figure. The close affinity of his thought with neo-Kantianism is most striking. It is apparent from his contact with Paul Natorp that he himself eventually became aware of this affinity. Both regarded philosophy as a strict science, both stressed the formal aspect of philosophy and both took human consciousness as their point of departure. The new element in Husserl's thought was his constantly renewed consideration of intentionality and it was precisely this which made his idealism doubtful as such and forced him to consider the problem of the concrete world in which man lives.

Husserl influenced not only the German philosophical movement known as phenomenology, which is so difficult to define and which has found its literary expression in Husserl's *Jahrbuch*, but also existentialism and neo-Thomism and, to some extent, the whole of contemporary philosophy. He has, too, had a considerable influence outside philosophy proper, in the spheres of jurisprudence, philology and literary studies, and still more in the spheres of sociology and psychology. The change of emphasis from genesis to structure is most noticeable in Husserl's thought and he played a leading part in enabling *Gestalt* psychology to find its form. His rediscovery, in his later thought, of the importance of historicity also made itself felt in the phenomenological movement in psychiatry and in the philosophy of Maurice Merleau-Ponty.

MAX SCHELER (1874–1928) was not a disciple of Husserl's, but he was certainly strongly influenced by Husserl's thought and philosophically closely related to him. Scheler's ideas also developed considerably throughout his life and this development was determined far more by the evolution which took place in the course of his own life than was the case with Husserl, the evolution of whose thought arose from the philosophical problems with which he was confronted. The development of Scheler's thought was above all influenced by his relationship with the Christian faith and the Catholic Church. The religious character of his philosophy was always very prominent. The central theme of his most important works was always man's involvement with the personal God of Christianity. In his last works, however, after his break with the Catholic Church, a pantheistic idea of God emerged quite clearly.

Scheler was not a systematic thinker like Husserl and most of the German philosophers. His books were always fragmentary, throwing light in different ways on various central problems. What is man? How is he placed in the world together with other men? What is his relationship with God? In attempting to answer these and similar questions, Scheler made use of Husserl's phenomenological method, but he did not concentrate his attention on this method as Husserl did.

For him, the method was simply a means of throwing light on and investigating man's essence. Scheler's manner of thinking was material, not formal. For this reason, he was unable to accept Kant's formal ethics of duty, but looked for a system of ethics which would propose to man values to be realized by him.

In his three most important works, Scheler dealt in turn with problems of ethics, of religious philosophy and of philosophical anthropology: *Der Formalismus in der Ethik und die materiale Wertethik* (1913), *Vom Ewigen im Menschen* (1921) and *Wesen und Formen der Sympathie* (1923). This does not mean that he discussed these problems systematically in a trilogy of books. The problems were, for him, closely interrelated. He was unable to separate ethics from philosophical anthropology and thus treated ethics as an aspect of anthropology precisely because he regarded ethics not as formal, but as determining the real values for man's being. Furthermore, anthropology was, for him, at the same time religious philosophy—the two could not be kept separate because all values were, in his view, directed by man's immanent orientation towards God. The present tendency to base the relative in the Absolute was one of Scheler's most powerful motives throughout the whole of his development as a philosopher.

Whereas Husserl was closely related, in his thinking, to the Marburg school of neo-Kantianism, Scheler was to some extent influenced by the ideas of the Baden school. There were, in Scheler's philosophy, the same emphases on the importance of values and the same tendency to view the sphere of values as a separate sphere alongside that of knowing and 'being'. But Scheler's perspective was more splendid than that of the Baden school. Whereas the neo-Kantians of the Baden school almost always asked questions within the framework of the theory of science, Scheler treated the theory of science as an aspect of his anthropology, which, in his case, had a religious orientation.

Man himself is not the creator of values: they prevail independently of him. Man's task is simply to recognize them and to realize them in the concrete. The formal ethics of Kant, who strove to reduce all moral activity to duty, cannot explain the phenomenon of ethics, precisely because he saw ethics as purely formal. It is, after all, not only a question of knowing *that* we have to do our duty, but also of knowing *what* our duty is. Moreover, duty alone cannot be sufficient, since love transcends duty and it is only in the case of love that there can be any question of ethics in the full sense of the word. The phenomenon of love directs our attention to a sphere which transcends that of the purely human. Love is always a relationship between persons. But there is, peculiar to the phenomenon of love, an impulse towards infinity which can only be valid in respect of man if he is more than simply man, in other words, if the finite person is related to an infinite Person, that is, to a creative and personal God. Therefore a really human philosophy is not possible unless this is ultimately related to God, just as, in the same way, a human action is not meaningful until it is ultimately related to God.

In his thought, Scheler gave very strong expression to the twentieth-century desire for philosophical concreteness. He firmly rejected the idea that science was orientated towards the concrete reality and philosophy towards the abstract, and insisted that it was precisely towards the concrete reality of man and the world that philosophy had to direct its attention. Without the world, however, Scheler maintained, man remained an abstraction. This attitude accounted for his interest in sociology. Man, he believed, had to be understood against the background of the world and, in this context, the I-thou relationship had to be investigated first of all. The questions which Scheler asked again and again were, for example, how does man stand with regard to his fellow man? How does man realize himself in his relationship with other men? How does man realize his involvement with God in and through these relationships? He thus gave expression and form to modern man's desire to turn inwards towards himself without losing contact with the reality of the world.

Like Husserl, Scheler had a very deep influence on European philosophy. Husserl's influence was felt mainly in the direction of formal reflection upon the method appropriate to science and philosophy. Scheler, on the other hand, prompted the development of a very rich theme which is still occupying the attention of philosophers, psychologists and sociologists even today. Finally, his work in the sphere of religious philosophy has had an influence on the religious problems and the revival of theology in our own century, especially within the Catholic Church.

In one respect, the influence of Husserl and that of Scheler were combined in NICOLAI HARTMANN (1882–1950). Like Husserl, Hartmann was a systematic thinker who used the phenomenological method so as to formulate and elaborate his ideas with the greatest possible clarity. The content of his thought was, however, to some extent formed by the problem raised by Scheler. But, because his philosophy left no room for a recognition of God, Hartmann 'secularized' Scheler's problem. He began with the neo-Kantianism of the Marburg school, but abandoned the idealistic point of view after reflecting about the central problem of knowledge and, partly inspired by the example of Scheler, came to accept a realistic concept of knowledge. Hartmann set out the fundamental ideas of his philosophy in his *Grundzüge einer Metaphysik der Erkenntnis* (1921), *Ethik* (1926), *Das Problem des geistigen Seins* (1933) and *Zur Grundlegung der Ontologie* (1935).

A phenomenological analysis shows that, in knowledge, subject and object are opposed to each other. The object determines the nature of knowledge. As such, it is independent of the subject and may, to that extent, be called a being in itself (*Ansichsein*). Both the real object and the ideal object possess this independence. This does not, however, imply that a choice has to be made between realism and idealism. Closer analysis shows that the phenomenon of knowledge is more readily made intelligible by realism than by idealism. All forms of idealism display inner contradictions. In the first place, the whole of man's natural attitude, which is always realistic, argues in favour of realism. In itself, of course, this is not conclusive proof of the validity of realism, but it is certainly true to say that idealism, whatever its form, is bound to provide an explanation for this original realism and this undoubtedly reveals a basic difficulty for idealism. The intentional character of knowledge is, moreover, extremely important and idealism cannot provide an explanation for this either. More convincing, however, than an analysis of knowledge is an analysis of human emotion. In many of our actions, we are emotionally involved with others and with things in the world. The reality of others and of the world is a necessary assumption for this involvement. The intentional character of knowledge and the reality of known objects do not exclude— on the contrary, they imply—the existence of an irrational element in knowledge. There remains therefore, in the object, something which is not accessible to knowledge.

Like Scheler, Hartmann allowed the objectivity of values to prevail in ethics. For him, the value also had a being in itself which was known by us, but could not be changed by us and there was a kingdom of values which had absolute validity. Together with the Baden school and Scheler, however, Hartmann made a distinction between the *being* of reality and the *validity* of values.

This is a question of human freedom. Freedom is not opposed to determinism. It transcends the antithesis between determinism and indeterminism. It does not do away with the operation of causality—it simply decides its direction.

Spiritual being cannot be defined in a completely unambiguous way. A distinction must, however, be made between the individual, the objective and the objectivized spirit. The *individual* spirit is man's spiritual consciousness, by which man is a person. The person forms himself in freedom. He is not completely determined by the situation in which he lives, but partly determines this situation himself. The *objective* spirit is the spirit of a definite society. The ideas and patterns of life created by the individual spirit can be taken over by others and, in this way, there is always a vital interaction between individuals. This objective spirit—the spirit of a definite society, for example—is not a person, but it has reality in the persons in whom it is present. The objectivized spirit is the legacy of the individual and the objective spirit in matter as displayed in reality and in particular in the sphere of art. In this objectivized spirit, a dovetailing of spirit and matter into each other takes place and this joining together is characteristic of human existence as spirit in reality.

The most important problem confronting philosophy is that of *being*—it is a problem that cannot be avoided. It is encountered not only in the most divergent sciences, but also in everyday life. It is brought to light even in an initial analysis of thought—we cannot think *nothing*, but always think something. Thus we always encounter at every turn what is, in other words, being. There is therefore a relationship between thinking and being. This, however, does not mean that being is completely merged with thinking. The distinction between the knowing subject and the known object always remains and the object is never entirely absorbed in the subject. There is, then, an element of irrationality in being which thought must recognize as such. This brings thought face to face with its most fundamental difficulty or *aporia*: because thought is necessarily related to being, but because, with equal necessity, it is impossible to penetrate completely into being, the last word of thought must be an admission of impotence. This admission should not, however, lead to our abandoning thought, since thought enables us to penetrate more and more deeply into being.

11. *Existential Philosophy*

The term 'existential philosophy' does not denote a clearly defined group of thinkers. It has, however, become fairly general practice to call such philosophers as Jaspers, Heidegger, Marcel and Sartre existential philosphers or existentialists, and it cannot be denied that there are characteristics common to these thinkers and those who are related to them. It is possible to distinguish two characteristics, one formal and one material, which apply to existential philosophy in general. The formal characteristic is that the word existence is not used in this philosophy in the classical sense, but in the sense of the human mode of existence, a usage which originated with Kierkegaard. The material characteristic is that, for existential philosophy, the problem of being is central and is approached from the vantage-point of man's being, which is seen both as something given and as a task. Existential philosophy can therefore be distinguished from other philosophical movements if these two characteristics are taken together. On the other hand, however, the extent to which various philosophical tendencies—neo-Thomism, the philosophy of the spirit and personalism, for example—have, in their later development, been influenced by existentialism also emerges quite clearly from these two characteristics alone. It is therefore not only difficult to draw dividing lines, but also not very important.

Existential philosophy, then, has developed the problem raised by Kierkegaard and Nietzsche in the nineteenth century. In considering this problem, existentialism tends to make use of the phenomenological method. More important, however, than these externals is the inner quest of existentialism. In what way is it connected with the twentieth-century idea of being? The paradoxical feature of this philosophy is that it reflects about concrete man in a concrete world, but expresses this reflection in very complicated abstract modes of thought. A further paradox is also closely bound up with this first one— these philosophers, whose thought is so 'technical', are often at the same time the authors of literary works which appeal to a very wide public. It is therefore only possible to gain an initial insight into existentialism by approaching it broadly from the point of departure taken by the existential philo- sophers themselves.

This is made all the more difficult by the existentialists' complete rejection of an unequivocal point of departure in the sense of Descartes's *cogito*. They also reject a broader point of departure in the sense, for example, of Husserl's consciousness. Philosophy, for the existentialist, is ontology. This means that the philosopher must ask why there *is* something. Why is there not nothing? If we are to know what *being* means, we must reflect about the experience of being that we ourselves have, or rather, that we ourselves *are*. We are, in the first place, always in the world—our being is *être-au-monde* (Marcel) or *in-der-Welt sein* (Heidegger). Our being is a being in the world and we can only understand ourselves from the world. Man discovers his consciousness as consciousness only when he returns from the world.

For the existential philosopher, then, the decisive questions are: What is the world? What is man? Who am I? What is being? Historically, these questions were prompted by Kierkegaard and Nietzsche. The existential thinker, however, only discovered them for the first time and became deeply concerned with them when the threat of his own age had made him ripe to consider them. Existential thought, then, has always begun as reflection upon the threat presented by the world. The two periods in which existentialism acquired its form were the periods which followed the two world wars. The impulse behind existential thought is the idea of catastrophe, of impending ruin and of threatening absurdity.

This does not mean that existentialism as such is a philosophy born of despair and moving back towards despair. Different existentialists have always taken a different attitude towards the threat of ruin. Heidegger's early work gives the impression that no other possibility is open to man than to have the courage to face up to his impending ruin. His later work, however, reveals a different perspective. Jaspers has, from the very beginning, always insisted that, in this crisis, everything depends on whether man can assume responsibility for himself. Marcel also shares this conviction, but, at the same time, takes an extremely serious view of the threat presented by objectivizing thought which is no longer conscious of its own limits. Sartre is deeply aware of the ineradicable absurdity of human existence, to which even death is of no importance.

This aspect of sharp and severe diagnosis is very prominent in existentialism, although existentialists are not alone in their diagnosis and prognosis of the human situation—historians like Huizinga and Toynbee and physicists like Eddington and Einstein have also made such diagnoses. But, from this idea of time, the existential philosophers have gone on to develop a characteristically profound and all-embracing philosophy. In this, the precariousness of man's existence is expressed in the existential idea: 'man exists' means that he realizes himself in a given reality. Thus, despite all the oppression of time, the idea of freedom nonetheless emerges. History does not make us—we make history. We are, however, not sovereign in our making of history—we are also determined by the history from which we live. Man and history live in a state of tension, which may be regarded as a vicious circle, but which is far more a spiral movement, through which man is able to act.

The same can be said of man's relationship with the world—man makes the world and is made by it.

It is clear, then, that existentialism is far removed both from idealism, which deifies human freedom and regards it as absolute, and from materialism, which denies this freedom or degrades it to the level of an epiphenomenon. The existent-ialists thus recognize that dynamism which characterizes man especially in the modern age—man's need to *plan* and his constant anticipation, in freedom, both of himself and of the present situation. Existentialism has, therefore, through this interplay of dynamism, freedom and determinism, been able to define a number of characteristics in which modern man can recognize himself. This is all the more possible because existentialism at the same time always regards man as individual and concrete and does not present him with an abstract scheme, but with a framework of possibilities within which he can situate himself in his own individuality and concreteness. This also accounts for the influence that existential philosophy has had on psychology and psychopathology, resulting, for example, in the work of LUDWIG BINSWANGER (b. 1881).

The existentialists do not, as the neo-Kantians and, to some extent, Husserl did, emphasize the structure of science, but stress man's being here and now in the world, in this way continuing the tradition of Kierkegaard and Nietzsche in the nineteenth century and of Bergson, Blondel and Scheler in this. Dilthey's historicism has enabled them to think of man as 'historical' and thus to abandon a rationalistic interpretation of man and the world. On the other hand, however, the existential philosophers avoid every form of irrationalism. They recognize the limits of man's being and thus of thought, and accept the mystery of this being, while at the same time rejecting any attempt to place the anti-rational systematically above the rational element.

It is very difficult to say where existential philosophy begins and where it ends. It is, for example, possible to speak of existentialism in the case of emigrant Russian thinkers such as LEO SHESTOV (1866–1938) and NICOLAI BERDYAEV (1874–1948) and in the case of such Spanish philosophers as MIGUEL DE UNAMUNO (1864–1934) and JOSE ORTEGA Y GASSET (1883–1955). All these thinkers have had an influence on European philosophy, but here it is necessary to limit ourselves to an outline of the work of those German and French philosophers whose thought has been decisive for present-day existentialism. In accordance with their conviction that man and the world are in a situation of crisis, existential thinkers in Germany and France have, on two separate occasions, produced some of their most significant work during an extremely critical period of history. The thought of Karl Jaspers, Martin Heidegger, Gabriel Marcel and Jean Wahl (b. 1888) was developed during the First World War and the period immediately following it, and the philosophy of Otto Friedrich Bollnow (b. 1903), Jean-Paul Sartre, Albert Camus (1913–1960), Maurice Merleau-Ponty, Simone de Beauvoir (b. 1908) and Paul Ricoeur (b. 1913) was similarly developed during and shortly after the Second World War. The Jewish religious thought of MARTIN BUBER (b. 1878) also shows some affinity with existential philosophy.

It would, however, be wrong to think that existentialism is simply a phenomenon of crisis. Crisis has impelled these existential thinkers to explore depths which would perhaps never have been discovered otherwise, but which throw light on aspects of man and the world which, quite apart from the critical situation, have real significance. This historical crisis has, in fact, once again raised the question of the nature of man's existence. If it has clearly shown the necessity of reflecting about man's being in categories different from those in which the being of things is considered, then this is obviously an insight that is valid independently of any situation of crisis.

That man is not a thing is no doubt a very old and inalienable human insight, but it is quite a different matter to draw ontological conclusions from this insight in order to understand reality.

It would be unprofitable to spend too much time considering what is common to all existential philosophy, since the differences are no less deep than the similarities. This is clearly shown in the fact that Marcel and Heidegger do not accept the title existentialist or existential philosopher, whereas Jaspers calls his thought 'existential philosophy' and Sartre calls his philosophy 'existentialism'. It is therefore preferable to bring these differences to light by means of a few examples drawn from the five thinkers who would seem to be the most important representatives of contemporary existential philosophy—KARL JASPERS (b. 1883), MARTIN HEIDEGGER (b. 1889), GABRIEL MARCEL (b. 1889), JEAN-PAUL SARTRE (b. 1905) and MAURICE MERLEAU-PONTY (1908–1961).

In his *Philosophie* (1932), Jaspers made a distinction between world orientation, existential illumination (*Existenzerhellung*) and metaphysics. All illumination of existence presupposes world orientation. Metaphysics is only possible on the basis of world orientation and existential illumination. World orientation takes place in the positive sciences and the practice of these sciences is the necessary condition for the practice of philosophy. This brings the philosopher face to face with the limitations of the positive sciences—he is confronted with many questions, none of which can be answered by the science concerned, but which nonetheless require answers.

The illumination of existence thus confronts us at the very outset with philosophical questions. The first of these is, what is existence? Existence is the realization of self in the world and thus at the same time the transcendence of this world. There is possible and real existence. Possible existence is the totality of conditions under which real existence can appear. Real

K

existence itself, however, is confined to those rare moments when man is able to transcend himself completely. Possible existence is not something universal or general like the positive sciences. Existence must be realized individually by each human being in his own distinctive way. Philosophy can only provide the general conditions for this. In the first place, existence is always historical: in other words, each human being is determined by the situation in which he lives. This situation is different for each human being. But no man can be satisfied if he is simply dominated by his situation. Man therefore asks questions which become particularly urgent whenever he is aware of being in what Jaspers has called a frontier situation, that is, a situation in which he is confronted with conflict, guilt, suffering or death. In such a situation man questions the meaning of his existence and does so in communication with others, since he is always essentially dependent on his fellow-man. It is only in communication with others that man comes to ask the most profound questions about himself.

This brings him to the sphere of metaphysics, in which man's transcendence of himself and the world is investigated. This transcendence occurs whenever man really exists. It can take place in various ways. Formal transcendence is the surmounting in thought of what can be thought. In the first place, my intellect compels me to transcend what is capable of being thought. Then I can come to myself in frontier situations and discover that I am intimately concerned with the transcendent, that is, with what is above man and the world. Then I can transcend man and the world by thinking about the symbols or *Chiffren,* as Jaspers has called them, in which man has embodied his transcendence throughout history. Then I have to seek to understand the language of myths and religion. The transcendent itself is inexpressible, but it can be indicated by the term God. Jaspers's idea of God has tended to become more and more theistic. Taking these basic ideas as his point of departure, Jaspers has, in his later work, placed increasing emphasis on an appeal to man to become aware of his responsibility for history in the present situation.

In *Sein und Zeit* (1927), Heidegger sought for the meaning of being. Before the philosopher can know what the question, What is being? means, however, he must find out what man, who asks this question, is. Man appears to be a being completely taken up with the world, a being concerned with things in the world and who acts, feels, wills and thinks as one acts, feels, wills and thinks. Concerned with the world and with other men who form part of this world, man (existence, or *Dasein*) can best be characterized as care (*Sorge*). This, then, is man in his everyday life. He thus has a certain concept of being. This concept, however, is pre-philosophical. It is implied in all man's activity, but it is not thematically elaborated. But is a thematic elaboration of this activity possible? Is it perhaps not true to say that man is so taken up with his everyday activity that he is incapable of thinking in any other way? He can, Heidegger maintained, only do so if he is torn away from his everyday experience by a special emotion, two forms of which are joy and anxiety. Heidegger closely examined the meaning of anxiety in *Sein und Zeit*. Anxiety takes man by surprise. It is not the same as fear, which always has a definite cause. Anxiety has no apparent cause—man is anxious about nothing. This shows that man, in his anxiety, is confronted with nothing. The whole of the industrious world, all beings, cease to exist. What remains is nothing. This nothing reduces all beings to nothing, that is to say, nothing shows the nothingness of all beings and of all human industry. Thus man discovers his own nothingness and therefore his real being, which cannot be recognized in his care for his everyday existence, his unreal being.

In his later work, Heidegger demonstrated that this nothing is the same as being. Precisely because it is not a being, being can only present itself as nothing to everyday man, who is accustomed to associate with beings. This therefore provides access to being. Discovery of being in turning away from beings fills man with joy. But what being itself is cannot be expressed. It is what makes a being be, but is itself in no sense a being. It is not the totality of beings, nor is it God, since God is above being. What it is cannot in any sense be expressed positively, but every human life and the whole of man's history are determined by the manner in which man is confronted with being.

Heidegger's philosophy is sometimes contrasted, as 'existential' philosophy, with 'existentialistic' philosophy, the name given to Jaspers's thought. This terminological distinction is based, on the one hand, on Heidegger's exposition of the existential structure, in other words, of the fundamental categories, of man's being as such and, on the other, on the call to man to come to himself made by Jaspers (and similarly by Kierkegaard and Nietzsche). Each man can respond to this call only in his own 'existentialistic' manner, that is, in accordance with his own individual existence. Jaspers's aim has been to investigate the meaning of this existence in the formal sense so as to point out to man various ways along which he, as an individual, can come to a realization of his own existence. However, although it has always been Heidegger's intention to define a universally valid ontological structure, he too has constantly stressed that existence means the existence of each particular concrete and individual person.

Marcel, fearing that any system results in a falsification of thought, has never constructed a systematic philosophy, but has always expressed himself in the form of diaries or in individual treatises on separate subjects. Both, for example, in his *Journal Métaphysique* (1927) and in his later Gifford Lectures, *Le Mystère de l'Être* (1951), his thought has always been a quest for man's being, in which it is clear that questions about man, the world, being and God cannot be separated. Man's being cannot be grasped unequivocally since it is characterized by the fact that it forms itself in spontaneous freedom. This does not mean that man should be thought of as being simply himself. On the contrary, it is only as a being in the world (*être-au-monde*) that man is. He thus always finds himself in a situation which is determined by his corporeality or incarnation. This situation is, however, not given as something which cannot be changed. It is partly subject to the influence of man who acts. In the world, man encounters other men and can have one of two attitudes towards them. The other person can be an object for me, just as a thing is an object, in which case the other is, for me, simply a 'he' (*lui*), or he can be a presence for me, in which case he is, for me, a 'thou' (*toi*). The 'I' forms itself above all the I-thou relationship, in which trust plays a decisive part. If I trust the other person and am faithful to him, then I create my own being. This trust, or *fidélité créatrice,* is, however, only possible because every 'thou' participates in the absolute 'Thou', God. Every man can, however, fall short, but God never falls short. Thus this creative trust is ultimately a participation in God's creation, a participation which is not passive, but active, because it is a constant giving of himself on man's part (*engagement*).

It will therefore be clear that Marcel regards philosophical thought as quite different from scientific thought. The positive scientist is confronted with problems which can, in principle, be solved and which therefore disappear once they have been solved. The philosopher, on the other hand, is confronted with mysteries, that is to say, with problems which can be clarified and into which he can penetrate more and more deeply, but which cannot be solved and cannot therefore disappear as problems. These philosophical problems thus, of necessity, constantly recur—they present themselves again and again in every period of history and to every human being individually. In this way, the problem of corporeality is, for example, a philosophical question—do I have my body or am I my body? It would seem as though my relationship with my body cannot be expressed either in terms of possession or in terms of identity. Corporeality itself, through which I am in the world, always retains the character of mystery. The same applies to our personal relationships with others and our involvement with God. Philosophical thought can throw light on these relationships, but cannot fathom them completely.

It is quite clear from Sartre's philosophical, psychological and literary works that his thought is of quite a different order. In *L'Être et le Néant* (1943), he discussed, like Heidegger, the problem of being. An initial phenomenological analysis reveals that there are two spheres of being—being in itself (*l'être-en-soi*) and being for itself (*l'être-pour-soi*). Being in itself is the being of material things. This being *is* without further definition. Being for itself is the being of consciousness. Consciousness is characterized by intentionality, that is to say, it is always directed towards the other. Indeed, it is even true to say that it is nothing but this orientation towards the other. This means that consciousness is always a consciousness of *not* being the other. Sartre called this reduction to nothing (*néantisation*). Outside this reduction to nothing, consciousness is nothing—it is the being by which *not* comes into the world. This also means that consciousness never coincides with itself. I can never identify myself with what I am *now*. I always transcend this and thus reduce to nothing everything that is in fact in me. This means that I am free.

Consciousness cannot coincide with itself, nor can it coincide with the consciousness of another. Everything that is called love is in fact a vain attempt at love. Either I make a thing of the other, in which case I no longer have any real contact with the other or I make myself into a thing so as to be dominated by the other, in which case there is also no real contact.

But consciousness not only wants to coincide with consciousness of the other—it also wants to coincide with itself, in other words, it wants to be at the same time both thing and consciousness. Since this is an ideal that cannot be realized, man projects it into the idea of God—God is, on the one hand, sufficient to himself like the thing and, on the other, pure consciousness. Therefore he cannot exist.

In his *Phénoménologie de la Perception* (1945), Merleau-Ponty attempted to consider the consequences of man's situation as consciousness in the world. If man is really orientated towards the world as consciousness by his body, there must be a spiritual and bodily unity in man and it must be possible to discover this unity in all man's actions. This means, then, that consciousness must always to some extent be corporeal and the body must always to some extent be spiritual. This in turn means that both empiricism, which recognizes only purely sensory perception, and rationalism, which recognizes only purely intellectual formation of concepts and deduction, must be rejected as methods of philosophical investigation. The method that must therefore be used is that of phenomenology if the phenomenon, man, is to be shown in his pure phenomenal form. Then it becomes clear for the first time that man appears neither as a thing nor as pure consciousness, but as a special form of being, of which consciousness and corporeality are aspects. Merleau-Ponty chose the sphere of perception to demonstrate this. Perception presupposes not only sensory corporeality, but also consciousness. There is, after all, no human perception without thought, just as there is no human thought without some form of perception. This unity of thought and perception throws light on man's ontological structure, which is unity in diversity. In his existence, which is spread out in time, man seeks to realize a unity which is before him as an ideal, but which cannot be realized in time.

All these philosophers, then, have been preoccupied with the same problem, but the answers that they have provided are only to a certain limited extent parallel with each other. They all share the conviction that man can only be understood as being in the world and that his freedom is a situated freedom. But even here, in connection with the problem of human freedom, they provide divergent answers. Is freedom the ultimate reality, so that man is there only for the sake of freedom? This answer made Sartre, for example, conclude that existence is absurd. Or is freedom there for the sake of man's togetherness with others, a togetherness which is possible because man is, in the last resort, involvement with God? This led Marcel to conclude that existence finds its meaning in love. For Sartre and Merleau-Ponty, the ultimate reality is man's dialectical relationship with the world. For Jaspers, Heidegger and Marcel, freedom pointed to a religious reality, which Jaspers has called transcendence, Heidegger salvation, and Marcel the absolute Thou. But the differences between these philosophers are not simply confined to their ideas about the meaning of life and the religious problem. Heidegger and Marcel, for example, have both attempted to overcome Descartes's dualism, whereas Sartre has taken this dualism to its uttermost limit in his division of being into the two spheres of being in itself and being for itself. The different attitudes taken by the existential philosophers towards consciousness are connected with this problem. For Sartre, consciousness has a Cartesian significance. Jaspers, on the other hand, speaks of it as existing in layers, while Heidegger avoids the word altogether as being historically too heavily charged.

It would, of course, be pointless to go into all the differences between the individual existentialists here. It is, however, of importance to bear in mind that existential philosophy is not a uniform phenomenon and that it even lacks the character of a school of philosophy all of whose members agree about fundamental issues. The differences are as basic as the points of agreement. All that these philosophers share is a certain climate of thought, a certain way of dealing with questions and certain fundamental insights. As is the case in all philosophy, existential thought has an aspect that is conditioned by the prevailing historical situation and an aspect that transcends this situation.

12. *Neo-Positivism*

By neo-positivism is meant the philosophical movement which originated in Vienna and is consequently known as the 'Viennese circle' of philosophers. This circle had ramifications in Berlin and Prague and was therefore not confined purely to Vienna. Various German and Austrian thinkers who formed a link with earlier positivism prepared the way for the work of the Viennese circle, and the empirio-criticism of the Swiss philosopher RICHARD AVENARIUS (1843–96) and the so-called thought economy of the Austrian ERNST MACH (1838–1916) anticipated the ideas of the circle. These two thinkers regarded philosophy as a theory of science, a general ordering and method of the sciences of which mathematics and natural science were the most pure forms. They were concerned with finding the most practical way of setting concepts in order so as to make reality as directly manageable as possible within these ordered concepts. Their ideas had a certain affinity with those of pragmatism on the one hand and with those of the French criticism of science on the other. The background to their ideas, however, was quite different. Whereas James's pragmatism envisaged a far wider sphere than the theory of science and had a background of spiritualism, the thought of Avenarius and Mach had an empirical background.

The Viennese circle tried to connect the empirical tradition with the new development in logic. The circle came into being in the nineteen-twenties under the influence of Wittgenstein's

Logisch-philosophische Abhandlung (Tractatus Logico-Philosophicus), first published in 1921. It became known through its programmatic publication, *Wissenschaftliche Weltauffassung: der Wiener Kreis* (1929). The circle's ideas have been variously termed as, for example, logical positivism and neo-positivism. Both these terms stress the similarities and differences between the circle's ideas and the positivism of Comte and Stuart Mill. While preserving the idea of empiricism, logical positivism at the same time sought to re-establish logic, though not by tracing it back, as Mill had done, to experience, but by fully recognizing its own reality, to which modern logistics had drawn attention. The two points of departure, then, for this philosophy were experience and logic. The relationship between experience and logic was at the same time one of the most fundamental problems facing neo-positivism.

The central figure of the Viennese circle was MORITZ SCHLICK (1882–1936). Other members of the group were HANS HAHN (1880–1934), OTTO NEURATH (1882–1945), HANS REICHENBACH (1891–1953) and RUDOLF CARNAP (b. 1891). The circle as such had a relatively short existence—its members were dispersed when Austria was annexed in 1938. The leading figures found refuge in England and America. This promoted the spread of neo-positivism, since English and American neo-realism was favourable soil for the neo-positivism of the Viennese circle, which exerted a deep influence on neo-realistic thinking for some time, in fact, until after the Second World War, when the English philosophers once again began to renew their links with their own original tradition.

Logistics should not be identified with neo-positivism. Just as logic in the classical sense is a method which has been applied by philosophers of widely divergent schools of thought, so too logistics is a method used by very different thinkers. Certainly, the Viennese circle argued constantly in favour of logistics as a method, but this did not result in all neo-positivists practising logistics. On the other hand, there have been many philosophers who have practised logistics without being neo-positivists—as, for example, neo-realists, neo-Thomists such as Bochenski and Feys, and metaphysicians with a Platonic orientation such as the German HEINRICH SCHOLZ (1884–1956).

The Viennese circle was a closely united group of like-minded philosophers, but, despite their basic unity, there were differences of opinion. A right wing, of which Schlick was representative, and a left wing, of which Neurath was representative, grew up within the circle, the left wing being the farther removed from traditional metaphysics. The contrast between these two wings became more pronounced with the years. It is of some importance to mention this division within the circle in passing, but, since what all these philosophers had in common prevailed in the long run, it is with this that we shall be concerned here.

These thinkers were, like the earlier positivists, radical and consistent empiricists. Unlike the earlier positivists, however, they firmly stressed the need to deal with what was empirically given in non-empirical logical thought and, in this, they were clearly influenced by the Marburg school of neo-Kantianism, by Husserl and perhaps above all by Brentano. In their radical rejection of metaphysics, they became the centre of philosophical interest and the cause of violent polemics. It was above all this negative aspect of neo-positivism that gave the Viennese circle, more than any other movement in philosophy during the second quarter of the twentieth century, the character of a school.

The most important works of the leaders of the Viennese circle, insofar as these are symptomatic of the thought described here, are: Schlick's *Allgemeine Erkenntnislehre* (1918) and *Fragen der Ethik* (1930), Carnap's *Der logische Aufbau der Welt* (1928), *Scheinprobleme der Philosophie* (1928) and *Logische*

Syntax der Sprache (1934), and Reichenbach's *Philosophie der Raum-Zeit-Lehre* (1928) and *Wahrscheinlichkeitslehre* (1935). The empiricist mode of thought of the members of the circle was closely linked with a strong English and American philosophical tradition and this became strikingly evident after they had left the continent and established themselves in England and America. From the very beginning, they were conscious of being within a definite tradition of Western thought. As early as 1929, Hahn stated this explicitly at the Prague congress: 'We acknowledge ourselves to be continuers of the empiricist movement in philosophy.' The logical method was elaborated above all by Carnap who, unlike the later logisticians, opposed the new logic to the older logic. His constant argument was that the older logic was unworkable, but that it was possible to assimilate all the empirical data in the new logical method.

The neo-positivists laid great stress on the principle of verification, although this principle appears to have been given various formulations. What it in fact amounts to, however, is that the significance of a judgement or statement (*Satz*) is determined by the manner in which this judgement can be verified. This verification is to be found in confirmation by empirical perception. All judgements which cannot in principle be confirmed by empirical perception are, in the literal sense of the word, non-sense, because no significance, no sense, can be ascribed to them. Only what can be confirmed by the facts can be meaningful, can have sense. Since metaphysical judgements can never be confirmed by the facts, they are meaningless, without sense. Verifiable is thus the same as true and reality is the same as the totality of the given facts. What is contradicted by the facts is untrue. But metaphysical judgements can neither be contradicted nor confirmed by the facts, so that they are neither true nor untrue, but simply meaningless, without sense, non-sense.

Although the neo-positivists insisted that it was possible to apply the logistical method to all empirical data, not all the neo-positivists practised this method. In the first place, these empirical data had, in the opinion of the neo-positivists, to be clearly established and a statement which unambiguously established an empirical datum was called a 'protocol statement' (*Protokollsatz*). There was, however, great divergence of opinion among the neo-positivists as to the nature and scope of these protocol statements. For Schlick, they were statements which possessed absolute and unquestionable certainty because theory and reality came into direct contact with each other in such statements. He preferred to speak of 'observation statements' (*Beobachtungssätze*), maintaining that protocol statements, because they contained hypothetical elements, belonged to a further stage.

Neurath, on the other hand, rejected Schlick's view, because he believed that expressions such as 'absolute truth,' 'unquestionable certainty' and 'reality' contained elements of metaphysics which in turn had to be rejected. For him, a protocol statement had a purely practical significance—it was based on agreement and on the inward coherence of thought, not on the bond between statement and reality. The hypothetical nature of a protocol statement therefore did not, in Neurath's opinion, detract in any way from its fundamental significance, since no statement could be anything else but hypothetical.

The philosophers of the Viennese circle were, moreover, convinced that a completely unambiguous scientific language was possible. Since all the sciences were concerned with the same basic facts, it was, in the opinion of these philosophers, bound to be possible to achieve a unity of all the sciences by means of this language. The sciences which had, in their view, made the greatest progress along this path were mathematics and natural science, but they also directed their attention to the other sciences and Neurath was especially interested in sociology. During the later stage of the development of neo-positivism in England and America, the same approach was used with many different sciences, such as biology, psychology and philology. An even later development, though connected with an earlier tradition, was the analysis of the ordinary language of everyday speech—but this, even when it was not simply rejected by the members of the Viennese circle, aroused very little interest among them.

Metaphysical statements are thus non-sense, because they cannot be verified. But there are also other spheres of linguistic usage in which statements are not verifiable. There are, in particular, ethical and aesthetic statements. Verification is impossible here because no facts are established in such state-ments—they only express evaluations. The same applies to *a priori* judgements in logic and mathematics. The necessity of these ultimate judgements in logic and mathematics is recog-nized, but they are only true by virtue of definition. They are what Wittgenstein called tautologies, in other words, they show what is implied in certain axiomatic assumptions. They do not themselves define anything, but they make it possible for us to pass legitimately from one definition to the other. Most of the members of the Viennese circle shared the convic-tion expressed by Russell and Whitehead in their *Principia Mathematica* that there is no distinction between mathematics and logic, so that all mathematical statements can be reduced to logical judgements.

Carnap stressed logical structure or syntax, from the very beginning, and within this structure he set down his ultimate rules (*Schluszregeln*) which defined the conditions under which one statement or class of statements followed as a result of another statement or class of statements. Syntax here is purely formal, the central concept being that of direct deducibility. This concept is not itself defined in its generality, but it has to be defined more closely as soon as a concrete syntactical system is constructed. Such a system can, like the whole of logic, be constructed as a calculation. For this purpose, Carnap made a distinction between proper and improper concepts. Proper concepts pointed to facts. Improper concepts, on the other hand, formed an axiomatic system. Many of the neo-positivists thought of these facts simply as physical facts, whereas for others, including Carnap himself during his early period, they were our experiences.

In the *Principia Mathematica*, Russell and Whitehead had reduced mathematical concepts to a few fundamental logical concepts. Carnap tried to do the same for empirical concepts in his *Konstitutionstheorie*, by elaborating systems in which, with the help of logical concepts, all empirical concepts were reduced to a few fundamental ones. In order to do this, he had to try to answer four basic questions. Firstly, there was the problem of the basis—what concepts could serve as the basis for the whole system? Then there was the problem of the forms of the stages—in what forms did the constitution of concepts from concepts of one stage to concepts of a higher stage take place? Thirdly, Carnap had to deal with the problem of determining the different forms of objects and finally with that of the form of the entire system.

In his book on the logical structure of the world, *Der logische Aufbau der Welt*, Carnap took man's own psychical experience as his basis or point of departure. Calling his approach that of 'methodical solipsism', he based the constitution of the physical world on the foundation of the subject's own psychical experience, the constitution of the psychical world of others on that of the physical world and the constitution of the spiritual world on that of the psychical world of others. Later, however, he abandoned this first basis of man's own psychical experience and took the physical world as his point of departure. Carnap was also convinced that he was not approaching this problem from a metaphysical point of view, but was simply making use of various ways of forming concepts and thus availing himself of the philosopher's freedom of choice.

The very different problem of ethics and aesthetics was one which interested Schlick from the very beginning. Once again, the point of departure was that ethical and aesthetic statements were not judgements about facts, but value-judgements. But, although the philosophers of the Viennese circle accepted that such statements did not provide knowledge, they also recognized that they could not be neglected. They did not, however, make much progress with this problem—a problem which tended to play an increasingly important part in later English and American neo-positivism. Schlick followed an older empirical tradition, treating ethical judgements as empirical judgements and regarding their validity as dependent on their relationship with human happiness. In this way, he arrived at a certain utilitarianism or eudemonism. Attempts to solve the problem in a different way led to ethics being treated sociologically and to the question of validity being ousted by the question of the manner in which man in fact forms a value-judgement.

The question of what philosophy really was for the Viennese circle and for neo-positivism in general is also of some importance. For the members of the circle, philosophy meant more or less the same as the logic of science. Philosophy had to analyse both the structure and the basic concepts of science. It did not therefore add any new knowledge to positive science, but threw light on it. It was not a question of arriving at a system of philosophical statements, but of clarifying the meaning of basic scientific concepts and logical methods. Wittgenstein claimed that it was impossible to speak meaningfully about language itself. Carnap, on the other hand, affirmed the possibility of a (symbolic) meta-language, constructed in logical syntax, in which it was possible to speak meaningfully about ordinary and scientific language. Schlick believed that the philosophy of the Viennese circle marked the end of the fruitless struggle between various philosophical systems. Like Wittgenstein, he regarded philosophy as an activity rather than as a system and consequently placed more emphasis on the practical philosophical treatment of problems than on philosophy itself. In this, he formed part of a whole philosophical tradition and was very much in accordance with other contemporary thinkers, however divergent their views may have been in other respects. 'The philosophical activity of giving meaning is the alpha and omega of all scientific knowledge'—this statement of Schlick's typifies neo-positivism in its first phase.

The views of the Viennese circle concerning philosophy were clarified by the question of apparent problems. The idea was worked out most fully by Carnap. All problems which could not in principle be solved logically and empirically were apparent problems. Thus, taken in the widest possible sense, all metaphysical problems—the nature of reality, the meaning of the world or of existence, the existence of God and the question as to whether the other's consciousness or an outside world can be known—were, for the Viennese circle, apparent problems. The members of the circle believed that it was meaningless to ask such questions, since the answers to them could never be verified. The answers were thus neither true nor untrue, but simply non-sense.

Most of the circle's later work was written in English and should therefore perhaps be dealt with under the heading of English neo-positivism. There are, however, two aspects of the later thought of the Viennese circle which cannot be included under this heading—Carnap's elaboration, during his later period, in association with the ideas of Tarski, of semantics, and Reichenbach's doctrine of probability. As these two very characteristic developments in the thought of the circle

L

did not take place in England, but in America, they must be considered here, since the final section of this book deals only with philosophy in England.

It later became clear that there was a need to amplify Carnap's view of logic as purely formal syntax, so that full consideration could be given to the meaning of the expressions used in scientific language. Three factors play a part in language—the speaker, the expression used and the meaning of this expression, that is to say, that to which the expression refers. A 'pragmatic' investigation is a full examination of these three factors. If, however, the first factor, the speaker, is left out of account and only the expression and its meaning are considered, this will be a 'semantic' investigation. If, on the other hand, the third factor, the meaning of the expression used, is also left out of account, what we have is a 'syntactical' investigation. Semantics and syntax can be examined both empirically and logically. In an empirical examination, existing languages—languages that are factually given—are investigated in 'descriptive' semantics and syntax. In a logical examination, on the other hand, artificially constructed languages are investigated in 'pure' semantics and syntax. In order to construct a language of this kind, a language, for example, which operates with symbols, it is necessary to use a meta-language, usually the ordinary language of everyday speech. These semantic investigations played an important part in later neo-positivism.

The second development referred to above was that of Reichenbach's view of the principle of verification. Whereas Carnap and most of the neo-positivists regarded the problem of the existence of an outside world as an apparent problem, Reichenbach did not. In this, he was far closer to the thought of the English and American neo-realists. He criticized Carnap for looking for absolute certainty where only probability could be found. If, however, we are unable to go beyond probability, the principle of verification must be formulated differently. We can say that a statement is meaningful if its degree of probability can be determined. In this context, there is more to be said in favour of the statement of the existence of an outside world than can be said against it. This statement is not only meaningful—it is also more probable than the statement that there is nothing other than our experiences. It is also more useful for the development of science.

The Viennese circle occupies a remarkable place in the philosophy of the twentieth century. In many ways, the members of this circle continued in the philosophical tradition of the nineteenth century, for example, in their empirical approach as philosophers who regarded empirical data as 'atomical', as Hume did, rather than as 'organic', as James did; in their exclusive recognition of mathematics and natural science as science; in their view of philosophy as simply and solely a theory of science; and in their rejection of metaphysics. On the other hand, their interest in logic gave all these aspects of their philosophy a quality of newness and, even though they were not alone in this, their influence on the renewal of logic has been very great indeed. Even their firm rejection of metaphysics has had a positive influence in that metaphysicians have been forced to give far greater attention to their use of language. It is possible to regard the 'narrowness' of the circle's views as enthusiasm for a new beginning in philosophy and it is also possible that these thinkers would have achieved a greater breadth of vision if they had been able to go on developing their ideas. The first signs of this broader vision were certainly present within the circle.

13. *Neo-realism*

There are very good reasons for reserving the term neo-positivism for the thought of the Viennese circle. It is, of course, true that this philosophy became widely known throughout the continent and the English-speaking world, but, in the process, its character underwent a change. The most remarkable aspect of this spread of neo-positivism was the contact that this movement had with the English neo-realism dating from the beginning of the present century. Long before the emergence of the Viennese circle, English neo-realism had, in reaction to the idealism of Bradley and Bosanquet, developed a philosophy which was, on the one hand, in keeping with the empiricist tradition of Hume, but, on the other, also took into account the later development of logic. In this way a philosophy was developed which was, in many respects, closely related to neo-positivism.

After the Viennese circle had been disbanded, several of its members made their home in England and exerted a neo-positivistic influence on neo-realism. For a time, there was a very great similarity between neo-realistic and neo-positivistic thinking, but, after the Second World War, the neo-realists gradually returned, with renewed insight, to their original tradition and their thought began once more to develop its own character. Certainly, the influence of neo-positivism could never have been so powerful if the Austrian thinker, LUDWIG WITTGENSTEIN (1889–1951), had not been closely associated, since his student days, with Russell and the environment of Cambridge. He had a very deep influence both on the Viennese circle and on later English neo-realism. He always, however, preserved a certain distance from the Viennese circle and felt much more at home in Cambridge. In any case, he played a mediatory part between neo-positivism and neo-realism, both by virtue of his *Tractatus logico-philosophicus* (1922), the bilingual edition of his *Logisch-philosophische Abhandlung,* published in 1921, and by his personal contacts and teaching in England from 1925 onwards.

English neo-realism, which was closely connected with American neo-realism, can be traced back originally to an article by GEORGE EDWARD MOORE (1873–1958), 'The Refutation of Idealism' (1903). Its close connection with the new logic can similarly be traced back to the early work by BERTRAND RUSSELL (b. 1872) and ALFRED NORTH WHITEHEAD (1861–1947), *Principia Mathematica* (1910–13). During the nineteen-twenties, Russell developed his logical atomism, which was also influenced by Wittgenstein. The influence of neo-positivism gradually became more marked until after the Second World War, when neo-realism again began to approach Moore's original intention more closely.

Not only a development, but also a divergence can be discerned within neo-realism. Moore not only preceded this divergence, but was outside it. Russell, on the other hand, has moved in a more positivistic direction, whereas Whitehead's thought had a metaphysical tendency. The later development in neo-realism has brought these two tendencies more closely together. In order to throw some light on this philosophical movement as a whole, a few representative examples will be given. Firstly, Moore's thought will be briefly outlined. Then Whitehead's ontology will be considered. After that, Wittgenstein will be discussed and finally a few words will be said about the latest development in English philosophy.

Other metaphysicians such as SAMUEL ALEXANDER (1859–1938) and JOHN LAIRD (1887–1946), the perspicacious analyst CHARLIE DUNBAR BROAD (b. 1887) and even such a forceful thinker as Russell must, however, be left outside the scope of this consideration, which is concerned with the problem itself rather than with providing as many different examples as possible. It is possible to consider neo-realism without discussing Russell, for example, because Russell's work in the sphere of logic, like that of Whitehead, does not fall within the framework of this book, because his work in the sphere of ethics shows little relationship with his basic philosophical idea of logical atomism, and because this logical atomism is in any case examined in connection with Wittgenstein.

Moore was a decidedly analytical thinker who wrote very little, but who had an exceptionally great influence in England and America. He believed that many philosophical problems were apparent problems which would disappear as soon as what was really meant by the problems had been precisely taken into account. What was above all required was an analysis of the terms used. As soon as the philosopher knew precisely what he wanted to say, and not until then, the second question arose—what arguments could be used to support this point of view? Moore was of the opinion that philosophers had frequently been very careless in their use of analysis and had not been exact enough in their handling of argument. This was, he maintained in his *Defence of Common Sense* (1924), one of the main reasons for the clear contradiction between so many philosophers and sound common sense. If a philosopher goes against common sense, he can only hold his own by seeking refuge in obscurity. Common sense is more reliable than obscure philosophy, but it is unable to defend itself. That is the task of analytical philosophy. Idealism, for example, was held in suspicion only because it is in conflict with the realism of common sense. The defence of realism, however, must be left by common sense to philosophy.

This idea led Moore to defend the ordinary language of everyday speech which philosophers so often disturbed. How difficult it was to maintain realism, common sense and everyday language consistently as philosophical points of departure emerged clearly from Moore's theory of 'sense-data', which was later adopted by Russell. Sense-data was the term which Moore used for the data of experience, acquired through the perception of some object. Moore did not himself realize that these sense-data were a theoretical product, since he was here still too close to an idealistic view of consciousness. The thinkers involved in the later development of analytical philosophy therefore looked for a more direct access to reality.

Moore's analysis preceded the divergence in neo-realism between positivism and metaphysics, although he did not, in principle, entirely exclude metaphysics. The idea that philosophy must always, in one way or another, be metaphysical was certainly present in his thought, just as it is in Russell's. The rationalist view that our knowing knows the known matter completely is not to be found in the philosophy of Moore, who believed that knowledge was capable of increasingly deeper penetration. The answer which common sense gives to the question as to what something is, is based on everyday experience. The answer to this question by science is based on the special scientific method. The answer given by analysis is based on the analysis of concepts and, finally, that given by metaphysics is based on the metaphysical system. Each answer thus penetrates more deeply than the previous answer.

Whitehead, especially in his *Process and Reality* (1929), gave an emphatically metaphysical direction to neo-realism. He began as a mathematician, but gradually turned his attention more and more to the central problems of philosophy. Every science makes use of abstractions, but there is always a danger of the abstractions of one particular science being applied dogmatically as categories to the whole of reality. Philosophy has therefore to take as its point of departure its own concrete intuitions. Neither the scientific method nor the historical method can be used in the case of philosophy. The philosophical method is that of rational reflection about experience, and experience here is wider than scientific and historical experience. Rational reflection enables the philosopher to discover the basis of experienced reality because reality, being, is in itself comprehensible.

This experienced reality, the world, is not an entirety of things. It is always moving and developing. The world does not consist of things, but of 'events'. (It should be noted in passing that this idea is common to neo-realism in all its forms and has a prominent place in the thought of, for example, Russell, Alexander and Broad.) The whole of the world is contained in every event, since every event has its roots in the past, anticipates the future and is related to the whole of the present world. Every event is therefore an organism. There are no purely external relationships—everything is related to everything else, so that the world is one great community. Whitehead's view of relationships is thus situated somewhere between Bradley's purely internal view and Russell's purely external view.

Idealism must be rejected because it cannot provide an explanation for the phenomenon of knowledge. All knowing is 'phenomenon' and contains a dualism, a relationship between subject and object, for which idealism cannot account. The phenomenon of knowledge also confronts us with the problem of mind and matter. Like Russell, Whitehead rejected the division between the psychical and the physical, between spirit and matter. This does not mean, however, that there is no distinction between them. We should not, with Descartes, regard spirit and matter as substances, but only as functions. There is a spiritual functionality and a material functionality and these are always so closely interrelated that any division between the two is impossible and it is even extremely difficult to make a distinction between them. In every event, however, there is a spiritual aspect and a material aspect. In the inorganic world, the spiritual aspect is not clearly apparent. In the world of man, however, it reveals itself in full clarity.

Metaphysics or ontology—like most of the neo-Thomists, Whitehead did not make a distinction between these two terms—is the science which gives, not the laws for a particular sphere of being, for example, for the world or for knowledge, but the universal laws that hold good for the whole of reality, for being as such. (Here, it should be noted, Whitehead was powerfully influenced by Plato: in the past, the whole of European philosophy consisted simply of commentaries on Plato's thought.) The present event can be understood by relating it to an ideal and 'eternal' object. These eternal objects are not really existing realities, but rational possibilities. The existence of reality itself calls for acceptance of the existence of God. Denial of the existence of God is bound also to lead to denial of the concrete reality.

Wittgenstein's *Tractatus logico-philosophicus* marked a climax in the philosophy of logical atomism advocated by Russell and at the same time an important step in the preparation for neo-positivism. It was a metaphysical treatise—the echo of Spinoza's *Tractatus theologico-politicus* contained in the title was no coincidence—which refused to acknowledge itself as metaphysical and yet attempted to reach unfathomable depths. The *Tractatus* was the last of Wittgenstein's writings to appear during his lifetime. It was only after his death that his *Philosophische Untersuchungen*—*Philosophical Investigations*—was published, that is, in 1953.

Wittgenstein himself summarized the contents of his *Tractatus* in the brief introduction to the book: 'What can be said at all can be said clearly and what we cannot talk about we must consign to silence.'[1] It is only possible to speak about what is the subject of the positive sciences. Philosophy in the traditional sense is therefore impossible. The only task that is left to philosophy, then, is to warn the philosopher whenever he goes beyond the limits of what can be said, in other words, the limits of positive science. Philosophy has no other task than this—to warn against philosophy. This does not mean that limits are set to thought, since, if this were so, we should have

[1] See Ludwig Wittgenstein, *Tractatus logico-philosophicus*, London 1961, 3.

to be able to think on both sides of this limit. Limits are only set to language, in other words, to the expression of thought. This limit is set by language itself—what lies on the other side of the limit is simply non-sense.

The world is the totality of facts, not of things. It is entirely determined by these facts and by nothing else. A fact is the existence of a 'state of affairs' (*Sachverhalt*). The state of affairs is a combination of objects or things. It is essential for the object to be able to be a part of a state of affairs. The logical picture of the facts is thought. Wittgenstein's statement, 'a state of affairs is thinkable', means that we can form a picture of it to ourselves. The totality of true thoughts is a picture of the world. Thought contains the possibility of what can be thought—what is thinkable is also possible. In a proposition (*satz*) thought is expressed in a sensorily perceptible manner. Only propositions have sense and a name or word has meaning only in the context of a proposition. A thought is a proposition with a sense. The totality of propositions is language. Most propositions and questions that have been written about philosophical matters are not false, but meaningless. Most philosophical questions and sentences arise from our failure to understand the logic of our language. All philosophy is a 'critique of language'. The proposition is a picture of reality, a model of reality as we imagine it. Propositions represent the existence and non-existence of states of affairs. The totality of true propositions is the whole of natural science or the totality of the natural sciences. Philosophy is not one of the natural sciences. The aim of philosophy is the logical clarification of thoughts. Philosophy is not a body of doctrine, but an activity. It has to define the disputable limits of natural science. It defines the limits of what can be thought and thus of what cannot be thought. It indicates what cannot be said by pre-senting clearly what can be said.

Propositions can represent the whole of reality, but they

cannot represent it in its logical form. This logical form is reflected in the proposition. The proposition *shows* the logical form of reality, which cannot be represented in language. For such representation, we should need a different language. What finds its reflection in language, language cannot represent. The sense of a proposition is its agreement and disagreement with possibilities of existence and non-existence of states of affairs. The most simple kind of proposition—what Wittgenstein called the 'elementary proposition'—affirms the existence of a state of affairs. One sign of such an elementary proposition is that no other elementary proposition can be in contradiction with it. If the elementary proposition is true, then the state of affairs exists. If the elementary proposition is false, then the state of affairs does not exist. The affirmation of all true elementary propositions describes the world completely. A proposition is a truth-function of an elementary proposition. An elementary proposition is a truth-function of itself. Elementary propositions are the truth-arguments of propositions. Truth-functions can be arranged in series—this is the basis of the theory of probability. The structures of propositions are internally related to one another. The truth-functions of elementary propositions are results of operations (Wittgenstein called these operations 'truth-operations') which have elementary sentences as bases. A truth-operation is the manner in which a truth-function arises from elementary propositions. Every proposition is the result of truth-operations on elementary propositions. *The limits of my language* mean the limits of my world. Logic pervades the world—the limits of the world are also its limits. That the world is *my* world is shown in that the limits of *language* (the language which only I understand) mean the limits of *my* world. The world and life are one. I am my world (the microcosm). There is no such thing as the subject that thinks or entertains ideas. The subject does not belong to the world, it is a limit of the world. No part of our experience is *a priori*. Everything that we see could also be different. There is no *a priori* order of things. This shows that solipsism, carried through consistently, coincides with realism. The self enters philosophy because the 'world is my world'. The philosophical self is not the human being (neither the human body, nor the human soul), but the metaphysical subject, the limit of the world—not a part of it.

The propositions of logic are tautologies. Therefore they say nothing—they are only analytical. That the propositions of logic are tautologies shows the formal—the logical—qualities of language, of the world. The propositions of logic describe the scaffolding of the world, or rather, they represent it. They have no subject-matter. They presuppose that names or words have meaning and elementary propositions have sense—this is their connection with the world. Logic is not a body of doctrine, but a reflection of the world. Logic is transcendental. Mathematics is a logical method. The exploration of logic means the exploration of everything that is subject to law. Outside logic, everything is accidental. What can be described can also happen. The world is independent of my will. Just as the only necessity that exists is *logical* necessity, so too the only impossibility that exists is *logical* impossibility. All propositions are of equal value. The sense of the world must be situated outside the world. In the world, everything is as it is and everything happens as it happens. There is no value *in* the world. If there is a value which has value it must be outside the whole sphere of what happens and is the case, since all that happens and is the case is accidental. What makes it non-accidental cannot lie *within* the world. (If it did, it would itself be accidental.) It is impossible for there to be any propositions of ethics. Propositions cannot express what is higher. It is clear that ethics cannot be put into words. Ethics are transcendental, like aesthetics. (Ethics and aesthetics are one.) It is not possible to speak of the will insofar as it is the subject of ethical attributes. If good or bad acts of will change the world, they can only change its limits, not the facts—not what can be expressed by language. This means that their effect must be that the world must become totally different. The world of the happy man is different from the world of the unhappy man. In the same way, at death, the world does not change, but ceases. Death is not an event of life: we do not live to experience death. If, by eternity, is meant, not infinite temporal duration, but timelessness, then the man who lives in the present will live eternally. Our life is as endless as our field of vision is limitless. The solution to the riddle of life in time and space is situated outside time and space. God does not reveal himself *in* the world. The mystical is not *how* the world is, but *that* it is. The mystical is the feeling of the world as a limited whole. The riddle does not exist. If a question can be asked at all, it *can* also be answered. There are, indeed, things that cannot be put into words. They *make themselves manifest*: they are what is mystical.

Wittgenstein's *Tractatus* ends with a reference to the relative nature of what is contained in it. This was, however, not scepticism on the author's part—scepticism is meaningless since it tries to raise doubts where no questions can be asked. Wittgenstein, however, suggested that his book was relative in that what he had said in it had to be transcended before a correct view could be obtained: 'My propositions serve as elucidations in the following way: anyone who understands me eventually recognizes them as nonsensical, when he has used them—as steps—to climb up beyond them. (He must, so to speak, throw away the ladder after he has climbed up it.) He must transcend these propositions and then he will see the world aright. What we cannot speak about we must consign to silence.'[2]

[2]*Op. cit.,* 151.

Very little can be said here about Wittgenstein's post-humous work. Whereas Moore insisted that analysis enabled us to penetrate more deeply below the surface, Wittgenstein argued that, in so doing, we ignored what was evident and lay on the surface. It was not, he maintained, a question of exposition, but of description. This description, however, was not made possible by passively perceiving, but by actively approaching the object from different points of view. Language, he said, was a labyrinth of ways—coming to a certain point from one direction, one might know the way, but, coming to the same point from a different direction, one might no longer know it. This idea was connected with the great emphasis which Wittgenstein placed on the ordinary language of everyday speech in his later work, an emphasis which did not occur in his *Tractatus,* but in which he fully supported Moore. Every proposition in everyday speech was, for the later Wittgenstein, in order as it was. Philosophy had no right to intervene in this everyday linguistic usage. Its task was simply to lead words back from their metaphysical significance to their everyday meaning. The movement from logical atomism to logical positivism and from analysis of scientific language to analysis of everyday language, which is, generally speaking, to be found in English philosophy, is reflected in the development of Wittgenstein's thought.

In the nineteen-thirties, analytical philosophy underwent a radical development which estranged it from Russell's atomism. On the one hand, outside influences, especially that of the neo-positivism of the Viennese circle, were responsible for this growth. On the other hand, however, there was also an internal development which brought to light the assumptions of logical atomism and exposed it as an arbitrary attitude. This internal development took place, in the case of Wittgenstein, between the publication of his *Tractatus* in 1922 and his *Philosophical Investigations,* which was edited by 1945, but not published until 1953. Wittgenstein's disciples and supporters in Cambridge were influenced by this, but a similar development also took place in Oxford and London.

It is impossible to describe this development in detail here or to discuss the work of individual philosophers. In broad outline, what happened was that logical atomism was abandoned in favour of a logical positivism closely related to that of the Viennese circle. This English neo-positivism, however, eventually began to reveal an inner insufficiency and gave way to a method of thought which no longer attempted to reduce everything to empirical or logical statements (tautologies), but tried to judge every statement in accordance with its use. Metaphysical and ethical statements were thus no longer classed *a priori* as nonsense. The idea gained ground that not everything could be categorized by antitheses, as verifiable or falsifiable, meaningful or meaningless.

In the first phase of this development, logical atomism was rejected as a metaphysical theory. Both the assumption of atomic facts and the assumption that facts were reflected in statements were postulated and neither resulted from the analytical manner of dealing philosophically with problems. Analysis had therefore to abandon tracing facts through statements. Its only task was to analyse the structure of language itself. This view was influenced by Carnap and was advocated above all by Ayer, who had for some years taken part in the work of the Viennese circle. The argument can be summarized as follows. It is meaningless to talk about things or facts. It is, for example, impossible to say, 'a rose is a thing'. All that can be said is, 'a rose is a thing-word'. Instead of saying, 'it is a fact that the rose is red', what has to be said is 'the rose is red is a statement'. It is equally pointless to insert 'sense-data' between the fact and the statement, since these can never be directly verified. A definition in sense-data is no closer to reality than any other definition.

In spite of this, the idea still persisted during the first period of this development that analysis could, in principle, provide every statement with an equivalent formulation which would be free from all the ambiguities of ordinary language, because the structure of language itself permitted a reduction from the composite to the simple. The possibility of reduction is, however, increasingly questioned in present-day analytical philosophy. A composite sentence cannot simply be reduced to a number of components. What is more, these components or simple sentences do not necessarily have the structure of communication at all. Questions and wishes or religious and metaphysical statements cannot be reduced to communications in the empirical sense, but to say that they are therefore without meaning is *a priori* reasoning. They are certainly meaningless as communications, but this does not mean that they are necessarily non-sense. The neo-positivistic view becomes, in principle, indefensible as soon as it is affirmed that every statement has its own logic.

It was, above all, the possibilities raised by the principle of verification which revealed the need for this development. What was the nature of this principle? Was it empirical or logical? It soon became clear that it was neither. It was, in fact, difficult to regard it as anything else but a metaphysical principle. But if this particular metaphysical statement was recognized as meaningful, it would not be proper to regard all other metaphysical statements as meaningless. Russell's conviction that philosophy could never entirely dispense with metaphysics was thus confirmed. The affirmation that the meaning of a statement lay in its method of verification thus appeared to be dogmatical by nature. This led to the idea that, in view of the fact that the criterion of verification ceased to apply, it was preferable not to seek the meaning of a sentence, but its use. The factual use made of questions and wishes or ethical and metaphysical statements was of greater importance to philosophical analysis than a principle which selected some statements and rejected others. This at the same time corroborated the classical English tradition in philosophy, as expressed by Hobbes, Locke, Berkeley and Hume, that the philosopher had always to return to the ordinary language of everyday speech and that everything that he could not express in that language was suspect.

It is difficult to name specific thinkers representative of this movement. The same philosophers who began as logical atomists later came, via neo-positivism, to this new understanding of analysis. One highly characteristic aspect of the whole development is the persistent conviction that philosophy is an analysis of language, despite all differences of opinion as to the nature of that analysis. Thus, Russell, Wittgenstein and Moore have played just as important a part in this movement as, for example, JOHN WISDOM (b. 1904) who called attention to the metaphysical nature of the verification principle, GILBERT RYLE (b.1900) who demonstrated the discongruence between grammatical and logical form, or ALFRED J. AYER (b. 1910) who was, for a long time, the leading representative of a logical positivism inspired by the Viennese circle. Analytical philosophy, then, has continued to develop, but, despite the many changes that it has undergone, analysis has remained the constant element. In one sense, the whole movement has been far more analytical in character than neo-realistic. There has indeed always been a danger, even in the case of Wittgenstein, that this philosophical tendency would remain enclosed within language itself, in a kind of linguistic solipsism.

The development of neo-realism is certainly one of the most interesting aspects of modern philosophy. After breaking abruptly with idealism at the beginning of the present century, this development has proceeded very gradually. It has been the inner problem which has led to this philosophy being

M

changed and deepened, with the result that it is possible to trace a constant line of development throughout the whole movement. The most constant line was undoubtedly drawn by Moore. The philosophy which moved away from Moore during the nineteen-twenties and thirties later returned to him. On the other hand, since the publication of the *Principia Mathematica,* Russell has behaved rather unpredictably with his repeatedly changing points of view and his frequently rash statements in the spheres of religion, ethics and history. Wittgenstein discovered, in the course of his development, what was already present, though latent, at the beginning of his career as a philosopher. Ultimately, then, he would seem to be closer to Moore than to Russell or the Viennese circle. Finally, Whitehead, among others, has shown how neo-realism in no way excludes metaphysics, an idea which has become widespread since the Second World War.

There is growing contact between English neo-realism and philosophy on the continent. Close contact could be important both for English thought and for continental philosophy. The sober and matter-of-fact English analysis could help to promote a critical examination of conscience on the part of continental philosophy, which is often in danger of losing itself in speculations which lack a firm basis. On the other hand, continental philosophy could also help to preserve English thought from a flat logical empiricism no longer aware of the really philosophical problems. German profundity, French clarity and English perspicacity ought to come together in a truly European philosophy.

4 Conclusion

1. *The Dialectical Character of Contemporary Philosophy*

Although twentieth-century philosophy shows a great diversity, it is not without an inner unity. Whereas the philosophy of the second half of the nineteenth century was materialistic and positivistic, that of the present century has been spiritualistic and metaphysical. This in itself expresses one of the tendencies of our own period—contemporary thought emphasizes not an either/or, but a both/and. It has not, except in an initial period of transition, opposed the materialism of the previous century with an idealism which denies matter, as nineteenth-century materialism denied the spirit, but with a spiritualism which recognizes both spirit and matter and asks questions about the relationship between the two. Both the problem of realism in the theory of knowledge and the question of dualism in philosophical anthropology have arisen as a result of this.

This both/and, both knowing and what is known, both spirit and body, is not, however, an eclecticism that, in the absence of any real power of thought, refuses to take up a position, but a distinctive mode of thought which goes back to Hegel and Marx in the nineteenth century and, even earlier, to Plato, and is usually known as the dialectical mode of thought. This sets knowing and what is known side by side, and does the same with spirit and body, as naïve realism did in the case of the first, and Cartesian dualism did in the case of the second, but at the same time views both in their indissoluble mutual unity. In the first case, there is the unity of knowledge which nonetheless displays a duality within itself—Husserl called this intentionality—and, in the second case, the unity of man which displays a duality of spirit or soul and body. The dialectical way of thinking is based on the unity within which is revealed a duality that, while developing, nonetheless remains within this unity.

This dialectical way of thinking is evident everywhere in contemporary thought—in physics, psychopathology and every other science as well as in philosophy. Twentieth-century philosophers have tended increasingly to think dialectically. In the first half of the nineteenth century man was, broadly speaking, regarded as free, and reality as a stable structure. In the second half of the nineteenth century, man was regarded as determined and *therefore* as not free, and reality as in continuous development and *therefore* as without structure. In the present century, philosophers have done away with this 'therefore'—man is now regarded as both determined and free, and reality as both developing and structured.

The first half of the nineteenth century was a period of theory and the second half a period of fact. Our twentieth-century way of thinking does not recognize any facts outside the framework of a theory or any theory that is not a theory of facts. The philosophy of the first half of the nineteenth century was characterized by its flight towards the absolute, whereas, in the second half of the century, philosophy tended to relativize everything. Twentieth-century dialectical thought, on the other hand, questions the relationship between the absolute and the relative. Also, while remaining conscious of the metaphysical and religious inspiration of the first half of the nineteenth century, it at the same time shares the awareness of the later nineteenth century that we are here and now in this concrete world.

Contemporary philosophy does not try to escape from dialectical tensions by withdrawing to one or other of the poles.

On the contrary, it is characterized by its constant attempt to think about this tension between two opposite poles as such. It is conscious that this is always the task of thought, so that thought is always capable of reaching a deeper level, since it can never fully understand. But this does not mean that all these tensions are always to be found within the same twentieth-century philosophical movement. Some tensions are apparent in the opposition between different philosophical movements. Thus, in irrationalism, the idea prevailed that the philosopher had to express his own personal being completely, without seeking universality—'subjectivity' was everything. On the other hand, Husserl in his early works, the philosophers of the Viennese circle and the neo-realists have tried to eliminate all subjectivity and to think only in terms of 'objectivity'.

Kierkegaard was above all the philosopher of subjectivity and the existential philosophers followed, in this respect, in his footsteps. They did not, however, like the irrationalists, accept subjectivity as something arbitrary. For this reason they have made use of the phenomenological method. The close association between the thought of Kierkegaard and Husserl, between existential thinking and phenomenology, which at first sight seems so unlikely, can be explained by the common attempt to include both poles in a dialectical tension. What contemporary existential philosophy has done from the very beginning has gradually taken place within English neo-realism.

This is most clearly discernible in contemporary thinking about language. Language is central in modern philosophy. The development of symbolic languages in mathematics and logic initially gave the impression that 'natural' language would become superfluous or at least only suitable for every-day usage. But it soon became clear that 'natural' language was a necessary and irreplaceable point of departure for all 'linguistic operations'. This was apparent to Moore at the very outset. It also partly determined Wittgenstein's development as a philosopher and was furthermore an important problem for Bachelard, Merleau-Ponty and the later Heidegger. Man is faced with the tension between 'creative' and 'received' language. He does not create from nothing. Rather, he re-creates himself and the world from the language that he has received as his mother-tongue. It is through this that he is formed and himself forms the world.

The tension between the two poles of united thought and action was the force behind the philosophy of Bergson and Blondel. In pragmatism, on the other hand, the pole of thought was only apparently less powerful than the opposite pole of action. According to Moore, analytical philosophy was of significance only in thought and not in action. In Marxism, however, the very reverse was true—thought was there only for action. Although this tension is not found in the ideas of some philosophical tendencies or individual philosophers, it is certainly to be found in the whole of contemporary philosophy. It is also apparent in the field of natural science and history.

Contemporary philosophy has also been aroused by the misery that modern man has had to suffer. The meaning of his existence has again become a vital question which man seeks to answer and the real problem of philosophy has thus once more been brought to the fore. But, in attempting to answer this question, the modern philosopher cannot take refuge in arbitrary fantasies—he is too aware of all the critical scientific investigation of the problem that has taken place in philosophy in the past. He sees metaphysics as a strict science which demands a total personal commitment. Philosophy, in its concern with its own problem, is conscious that it is closely associated with and at the same time distinct from religion, art and science. But it knows that it must always be concerned with the whole man and philosophy today is animated by this grave preoccupation.

INDEX

TWENTIETH CENTURY PHILOSOPHY

Bernard Delfgaauw

This book was written to meet the widely-felt need for a clear account of the very complex and diversified movement of philosophy in the present century. In the course of twenty chapters the author explains the background, the influence of tradition and the radically new insights of the philosophy of our time.

With a remarkable mastery of his subject he provides a splendid introduction to the fundamental themes of philosophies such as Neo-Hegelianism, Marxism, Pragmatism, Neo-Thomism, Personalism, Phenomenology, Existentialism and Neo-Positivism.

A particularly valuable feature of the book is the manner in which Professor Delfgaauw indicates the inter-relationships which are found between the various currents of contemporary philosophy. He enables the reader to discern common interests and orientations at work throughout the immensely varied landscape of modern philosophical thinking.

The author carries his learning lightly; this is a very readable book. It will be welcomed not only by students of philosophy, but by all who are interested in a better understanding of the intellectual climate of our time.